ENGLISH

Communicative

QUESTION-ANSWERS

ENGLISH

Communicative

CLASS 9th

by
Raina Jain

ARIHANT PRAKASHAN, MEERUT

ARIHANT PRAKASHAN, MEERUT

Administrative & Production Offices

Corporate Office: 'Ramchhaya' 4577/15, Agarwal Road, Darya Ganj, New Delhi -110002
Tele: 011- 47630600, 43518550; Fax: 011- 23280316

Head Office: Kalindi, TP Nagar, Meerut (UP) - 250002
Tele: 0121-2401479, 2512970, 4004199; Fax: 0121-2401648

All disputes subject to Meerut (UP) jurisdiction only.

Sales & Support Offices

Agra, Ahmedabad, Bengaluru, Bhubaneswar, Bareilly, Chennai, Delhi, Guwahati, Haldwani Hyderabad, Jaipur, Jalandhar, Jhansi, Kolkata, Kota, Lucknow, Meerut, Nagpur & Pune

ISBN 978-93-5141-565-7

Typeset by Arihant DTP Unit at Meerut

For further information about the products from Arihant
log on to **www.arihantbooks.com** or email to **info@arihantbooks.com**

Preface

Feeling the immense importance and value of NCERT books, we are presenting this book, having the **NCERT Exercises Solutions.** For the overall benefit of the students we have made this book unique in such a way that it presents not only solutions but also detailed explanations. Through these detailed and through explanations, students can learn the concepts which will enhance their thinking and learning abilities.

Explanatory Solutions have been provided to all the questions given in each chapter of NCERT book. We have given all the points that tell how to approach to solve a problem. Here we have tried to cover all those loopholes which may lead to confusion. All formulae and hints are discussed in full detail.

Apart from all those who helped in the compilation of this book a special note of thanks to Ms Rakhi Rasniya and Ms Madhumita Pattrea. With the hope that this book will be of great help to the students, I wish great success to my readers.

Raina Jain

Contents

Term I

Fiction

Poetry

Drama

Term II

Fiction

Poetry

Drama

Term I

Fiction

1

How I Taught My Grandmother to Read

Sudha Murty

Synopsis

'How I Taught My Grandmother to Read' is a story written by Sudha Murty that reveals the determination and hard work of a sixty-two year-old lady Krishtakka to become literate and independent. The narrator, the granddaughter of Krishtakka, used to read the episodes of the novel 'Kashi Yatre' to her every week from the weekly magazine 'Karmaveera'. Being illiterate, Krishtakka was unable to read herself. Later on, her desire to be self dependent and literate and her amazing determination made her able to read books.

Detailed Summary

The Narrator With Her Illiterate Grandmother in the Village

The narrator is a twelve-year-old little girl who introduces herself. She lived in a village of North Karnataka with her grandparents. The narrator's grandmother was an illiterate lady who was fond of the novel 'Kashi Yatre' written by Triveni, the famous Kannada novelist.

Triveni's Novel and its Characters; An Old Lady and An Orphan Girl

'Kashi Yatre' was being released in serial form in the Kannada weekly 'Karmaveera', a popular magazine. Most of the villagers were fond of it, including the little girl's grandmother. 'Kashi Yatre' is a story of an old lady and her ardent desire to go to Kashi or Varanasi. Most of the Hindus believe that going to Kashi and worshipping Lord Vishweshwara is the ultimate punya. The author's grandmother also believed in this and therefore she used to compare herself with the protagonist of the novel.

In the story 'Kashi Yatre', there was also a young orphan girl who falls in love but had no money for the wedding. In the end, the old lady gave away all her savings for the wedding of the orphan girl without going to Kashi.

The Narrator Reads the Story to Her Grandmother

The old lady, Krishtakka, used to hear the story from the author with great concentration and interest. Later, she could repeat the entire text by heart. She used to discuss the latest episode with her friends at the temple.

Grandmother's Reaction to the Narrator's Absence

Once the author had to go for a wedding with her cousins to the neighbouring village. She stayed there for a week. When she returned, she found her grandmother in tears.

Grandmother Relates Her Life Story and Ambition to be Literate

Her grandmother told her that when she was a young girl, she lost her mother. Her father got married again and she was also married very young and had children. She never got the chance to study or go to school. She said that she made sure that her children and grandchildren studied well.

She told her granddaughter that now at the age of sixty-two, she wanted to study and become independent. At first the little girl made fun of her grandmother, but later on she realised her determination and will power. Her grandmother proved herself an excellent student and learnt to read Kannada language within the decided deadline, till Dasara festival.

Grandmother's Gesture to Her Guru

On Dasara festival, the little girl bought the novel 'Kashi Yatra' as a gift for her grandmother. Her grandmother also gifted her some frock material, and touched the feet of her granddaughter. She said that she was not touching the feet of her granddaughter, rather she was paying her respects to a teacher which is an essential part of our culture.

About the Author

Sudha Murty was born in Shiggaon in north Karnataka. A prolific writer in Kannada, she has written seven novels, four technical books, three travelogues and two collections of short stories. Her English book 'Wise and Otherwise has been translated into thirteen Indian languages. Her stories deal with common lives and human values such as charity, kindness and self-realisation. As a sensitive writer, she writes about the suffering of the people. The main characters in all her books are highly educated, non-compromising, highly principled women.

Exercises

Question 1. Write about the following memories or experiences. Share your views with the class.

(i) A memorable holiday spent with your grandmother

Answer **A Memorable Holiday Spent with My Grandmother** Yes, I can never forget the memorable holiday, I spent with my grandmother last week. Our school was closed for autumn break, my parents had to go out of the city so they called my grandmother at our place as I was all alone. I was very excited, overjoyed to see my grandmother. She hugged me and gave some nice gifts. She cooked delicious dishes for me.

She narrated all kinds of moral stories to me. She asked me to pray to God for prosperity of all. She advised me to be honest and hard working. She told me that man's good deeds make him great. She also told me to love poor and needy people. All her teachings had an indelible impression on me. I promised my grandmother to follow her advice in my life.

(ii) A story told by your grandmother

Answer **A Story Told by My Grandmother** My grandmother told me a story of a dog who was very greedy. Oneday he had found a large piece of meat and was carrying it away in his mouth, so he could eat it in peace somewhere. He came to a stream and began to cross over a narrow plank which led him from one bank to the other. Suddenly, he stopped and looked down.

In the water he saw his own reflection. The dog did not realise he was looking at himself. He thought he was looking at another dog with a large piece of meat in his mouth. He wanted to snatch the piece of meat thinking it bigger and dropped his own piece of meat in the stream. The dog learnt a bitter lesson of not to be greedy.

(iii) The things you admire the most about your grandmother

Answer **The Things I Admire the Most About My Grandmother** My grandmother has many good qualities. She is all in one. My grandmother is simple, honest and hard working. She has a great faith in God. She is an early riser and completes all her tasks in time. She is active and does all the work herself.

She is a very good cook and advices us to eat healthy and delicious food. She always helps the poor and needy people. Due to her these qualities she is liked, loved and respected by all. I love my grandmother and proud to be her granddaughter.

(iv) The difference between your mother and your grandmother

Answer **The Difference Between My Mother and My Grandmother** Yes, there is much difference between my mother and my grandmother. It is mainly because of her being in service. My mother has less time and is always in a hurry. She does not have enough time to spend with us or cook food for us.

Although, she loves us, but sometimes she becomes very strict. She is unable to tell stories like grandmother. But my grandmother strongly believes in love and affection. My grandmother says that giving moral values can bring wonderful results.

Question 2. Now that you have enjoyed reading the story, answer the following questions by choosing the correct option.

(a) The grandmother could relate to the central character of the story 'Kashi Yatre' as

(i) both were old and uneducated
(ii) both had granddaughters who read to them
(iii) both had a strong desire to visit Kashi
(iv) both were determined to learn to read

Answer (iii) Both had a strong desire to visit Kashi

(b) Why did the women at the temple discuss the latest episode of 'Kashi Yatre'?

(i) To pass their time
(ii) The writer, Triveni was very popular
(iii) They could relate with the protagonist of the serial
(iv) Women have a habit of discussing serials

Answer (iii) They could relate with the protagonist of the serial

(c) The granddaughter found her grandmother in tears on her return as

(i) the grandmother had been unable to read the stroy 'Kashi Yatre' on her own
(ii) the grandmother had felt lonely
(iii) the grandmother wanted to accompany her granddaughter
(iv) she was sad she could not visit Kashi

Answer (i) The grandmother had been unable to read the story 'Kashi Yatre' on her own

(d) Why did the grandmother touch her granddaughter's feet?

(i) As a mark of respect to her teacher
(ii) It was a custom in their family
(iii) Girls should be respected
(iv) She had read the story of 'Kashi Yatre' to her

Answer (i) As a mark of respect to her teacher

Question 3. Answer the following questions briefly

(a) What made Triveni a popular writer?

Answer Triveni was a very popular and wonderful writer in the Kannada language. Her style was easy and convincing. Her stories usually dealt with complex psychological problems in the lives of common men and were always very interesting. The readers identified themselves with the characters of her stories hence it made her a popular writer.

(b) Why did the grandmother depend on her granddaughter to know the story?

Answer The grandmother was dependent on her granddaughter to know the story because she was illiterate. She lost her mother at an early age so there was no one to guide her. Infact her granddaughter used to read the story for her.

(c) Pick out two sentences which state that the grandmother was desperate to know what happened in the story.

Answer The two sentences are

(i) 'Many times, I rubbed my hands over the pages wishing they could understand what was written'.

(ii) 'I even thought of going to the village and asking you to read for me.'

(d) Could the grandmother succeed in accomplishing her desire to read. How?

Answer Yes, the grandmother succeeded in accomplishing her desire to read. Her granddaughter made her read, write and recite each of the alphabets. She taught her with great affection and made her independent.

(e) Which of the following traits would be relevant to the character of the narrator's grandmother?

(i) determined
(ii) selfish
(iii) emotional
(iv) mean

Give reasons for your choice.

Answer The narrator's grandmother is a determined and emotional lady. Her determination can be judged when she learnt to read Kannada language even at the age of sixty-two in a short span of time.

The grandmother showed her emotional side when she cried on her inability to read and write. This showed her simplicity and desperate willingness to learn.

Question 4. Here are some direct quotations from the story. Identify the speaker and write what each quotation suggests about the speaker. You can use the adjectives given in the box and may also add your own.

amiable, tender, gentle, sympathetic, understanding, determined, diligent, kind, concerned, systematic, wise, helpful, enthusiastic, selfish, cruel, humble, religious, prudent.

Speaker	Quotation	Quality Highlighted
	'Avva is everything all right? Are you OK?'	
	'At times, I used to regret not going to school, so I made sure that my children and grandchildren studied well.'	
	'Avva, don't cry. What is the matter? Can I help you in anyway?'	
	'We are well-off, but what use is money when I cannot be independent.'	
	'I will keep Saraswati pooja day during Dassara as the deadline'.	
	'For a good cause if you are determined you can overcome any obstacle'.	
	I am touching the feet of a teacher not my granddaughter.	

Answer

Speaker	Quotation	Quality Highlighted
Narrator	'Avva is everything all right? are you OK?'	Amiable, kind, understanding, concerned sympathetic, wise, intelligent
Grandmother	'At times, I used to regret not going to school, so I made sure that my children and grandchildren studied well.'	Prudent, mature, understanding, wise
Narrator	'Avva, don't cry. What is the matter? Can I help you in anyway?'	Tender, co-operative helpful, kind
Grandmother	'We are well-off, but what use is money when I cannot be independent.'	Understanding, thoughtful, diligent, pragmatic far-sighted
Grandmother	'I will keep Saraswati pooja day during Dassara as the deadline'.	Determined, religious, systematic decisive
Grandmother	'For a good cause if you are determined you can overcome any obstacle'.	Determined, diligent enthusiastic, wise
Grandmother	I am touching the feet of a teacher not my granddaughter.	Cultured, prudent, amiable tender, religious, mature

Question 5. After having read the story, you realise the anguish of the illeterate adults, You want to make your friends aware of it and contribute something in bringing about a change in the lives of illiterate adults. Deliver a speech in the morning assembly at your school about the importance of adult-education and ways to implement it.

Answer

Good morning everyone,

We all know that education enlightens and empowers. In a developing country like ours, about half of the population is illiterate. They are liable to be cheated everywhere. They have to be dependent on others for knowing things, they cannot join the mainstream of social life. What we need to do is to follow the slogan in true spirit 'Each one teach one'.

The literacy programmes can be fruitful if we support the programmes wholeheartedly. We can hold these camps in villages and tell the villagers the advantages of being literate. Literate women can bring drastic changes in their lives. They can read material on child care, health and hygiene, and other areas of human knowledge. They can progress in all fields of life. They can decide what is good and bad for them. We should convince them to join the literacy classes.

Thank you.

Writing Task

Question 6. You are the grandmother. How did you feel when your granddaughter gave you the novel 'Kashi Yatre'? Write your feelings in your diary.

Answer

7th March, Thursday, 20 xx 9 pm

Today I am very happy as my granddaughter gave me the novel 'Kashi Yarte' which I can now read myself. When she gave me the book, I became very happy as it was my favourite novel. It is because my grand daughter's devotion and love that I am able to read and write myself. She made me independent. Now, I donot have to wait for anybody to read and write for me. My life long dream of being a literate has come true. Actually I am very fond of this novel.

When it was serially published in live Kannada weekly Karmaveera. I became interested in knowing more about the old lady. I identified myself with his lady. I also wanted to go to Kashi and thought that worshippy Lord Vishweshwara was the ultimate punya. I fully supported the old lady when she gave all her money for the wedding of the poor orphan girl.

I believed that this generous act of the lady gave her more punya. I really love this novel as it is first novel which inspired me to be literate and independent. Many sweet memories are intermined with this novel. I cannot forget how I doveloped a deep for the old lady of this novel and how my granddaughter became my teacher. It is really special tome.

Question 7. Here is a story about Swami and his grandmother. After reading the excerpt, change it into a conversation between Swami and his grandmother.

After the night meal with his head on his Granny's lap, nestling close to her, Swaminathan felt very snug and safe in the faint atmosphere of cardamom and cloves.

'Oh, Granny!' he cried ecstatically. 'You don't know what a great fellow Rajam is.' He told her the story of the first enmity between Rajam and Mani and the subsequent friendship.

'You know, he has a real police dress,' said Swaminathan.

'Is it? What does he want a police dress for?' asked Granny.

'His father is the Police Superintendent. He is the master of every policeman here.'

Granny was impressed. She said that it must be a tremendous office indeed. She then recounted the days when her husband, Swaminathan's grandfather, was a powerful sub-magistrate, in which office he made the police force tremble before him and the fiercest dacoits of the place flee. Swaminathan waited impatiently for her to finish the story. But she went on, rambled, confused, mixed up various incidents that took place at different times. 'That will do, Granny,' he said ungraciously. 'Let me tell you something about Rajam. Do you know how many marks he gets in arithmetic?'

'He gets all the marks, does he, child?' asked Granny.

'No silly. He gets ninety marks out of one hundred.'

'Good, But you must also try and get marks like him.... You know, Swami, your grandfather used to frighten the examiners with his answers sometimes. When he answered a question, he did it in a tenth of the time that others took to do it. And then, his answers would be so powerful that his teachers would give him two hundred marks sometimes.

'Oh, enough, Granny! You go on bothering about old unnecessary stories. Won't you listen to Rajam?'

'Yes, dear, yes.'

'Granny, when Rajam was a small boy, he killed a tiger.'

Swaminathan started the story enthusiastically: Rajam's father was camping in a forest.

He had his son with him. Two tigers came upon them suddenly, one knocking down the father from behind. The other began chasing Rajam, who took shelter behind a bush and shot it dead with his gun.

'Granny, are you asleep?' Swaminathan asked at the end of the story.

Now read the dialogue and complete the conversation

Swami	You don't know what a great fellow Rajam is! In the beginning I could not get along with him but now he is my good friend. And you know, he has a real police dress.
Grandmother	Is it? What does he want a police dress for?
Swami	His father is the Police Superintendent. He is the master of every policeman here.
Grandmother	I think, it must be a tremendous office. Do you know, your grandfather was a powerful sub-magistrate and the Police Force trembled before him? Even the fiercest dacoits of the place fled.

Swami That will do, Granny. It's so boring. Let me tell you something about Rajam. Do you know how many marks he gets in arithmetic?

Grandmother He gets all the marks doesn't he, child?

Answer

Swami 'Oh, Granny! my fellow Rajam is really a fabulous person. He is very brave and intelligent. He also understands the value of friendship.

Earlier, we were not good friends as I was unable to understand him. He is an open heart person. He also keeps a real police dress at his home.

Granny Is it really true? If it is true then why does he keep a police dress with him?

Swami His father is the police superintended and he controls all the police men in this area.

Granny I believe that his office must be tremendous. Your grandfather was also a powerful sub-magistrate in which office he made the police force tremble before him and the fiercest dacoit of the place flee. He was the owner of an impressive personality.

Swami Sounds good, Granny. Let me tell you that my fellow. Rajam is excellent in study also. Do you know how many marks he gets in arithmetic?

Granny I think he gets all the marks, does he.

Swami No, silly. He achieves 90 per cent marks in the subject.

Granny That's ok. But you should also do the same. You know, Swami your grandfather used to frighten the examiners with his answers sometimes. When he answered a question he took one tenth of the time that others took. Sometimes his answers would be so powerful that his teachers would give him two hundred marks.

Swami Oh, enough, Granny! You relate unnecessary stories. Would you please listen about Rajam?

Granny It's ok. You can continue.

Swami Once, Rajam and his father were camping in a forest. Suddenly, two tigers attacked on them. One of them knocking down his father from behind. The other tiger begam chasing Rajam, who took shelter behind a bush and shot it dead with his gun.

(Swami finds his grandmother sleeping)

Swami Are you sleeping, Granny.

Oh! Granny, it is not good of you.

2

A Dog Named Duke

William D Ellis

Synopsis

'A Dog Named Duke' is a story written by William D Ellis. It is a story about a dog named Duke who transformed the life of his master Chuck Hooper. Chuck Hooper's body was paralysed due to an accident. With the support of Duke, Chuck Hooper was able to recover and become physically fit. He was promoted professionally also as an Assistant National Sales Manager. But Duke met a fatal accident and died at the end of the story.

Detailed Summary

About Charles Hooper

Duke was a rough playing Doberman Pinscher, four years old and weighed 23 kilos. Chuck Hooper bought him. However, his wife Marcy did not like the dog. It took a long time for Marcy to get used to the dog. Chuck Hooper was a smart young man. He was cheerful, physically fit and a professionally settled man.

Chuck is Paralysed in An Accident

Suddenly, he met with an accident and the left part of his body was completely paralysed. He was working as a successful Zone Sales Manager. Due to his injury, his company decided to give him a year's leave from duty. Later on, a desk job would be created for him at headquarters as he could not move around.

Chuck's Boring Life on Returning from Hospital

Life became lonely for Chuck as his wife used to go for her job and he was left alone for the whole day. His dog Duke was brought home from the kennel. When Duke came, he expressed his joy by springing on his master Chuck Hooper. Chuck could hardly keep his balance. From then onwards Duke took up his position near Chuck's bed and never jumped on him, as if he understood everything.

Duke Helps Chuck to Start Walking

Slowly, with the help of Duke and Marcy, one day Chuck took one step. However, he collapsed on the wheelchair after this. Next day, Duke nudged Hooper's good side again to move. That day Chuck took four steps. Slowly, Chuck learned to balance his body without Marcy. Taking steps and increasing them day by day, Duke and Chuck reached the front porch.

Neighbours saw Duke struggling with Chuck every day. Duke would pull his leash, stand and wait. Chuck would drag himself abreast of the dog. Very soon Chuck was able to walk. Marcy told the doctor about Chuck's progress and he prescribed a course of physiotherapy for him along with walking every day with Duke. Soon Duke and Chuck would make two trips a day.

Chuck Starts Working Again

After March, Chuck did not need the physiotherapy and went to office. With the help of Duke, Chuck was improving his stability and endurance. At the job, Chuck started working well and he was promoted as Regional Manager.

On 1 March, 1956 Chuck, Marcy and Duke moved to a new house where people did not know what Duke had done for his master. All they knew was that Chuck walked like a mechanical giant and the dog pulled him as if he owned him.

Duke Dies in Accident; Given a Tribute

After about nine months, Duke met with an accident. Marcy took Duke to an animal hospital but could not save him. Later Chuck received a letter from his company for his promotion as Assistant National Sales Manager. Chuck felt that this promotion was a tribute to Duke.

About the Author

William D. Ellis was an author born in Concord, Massachusetts, USA. He began writing at the age of 12, at the urging of an elementary school teacher who early on discerned his talent. Ellis's study of the history of Ohio provided him material that he eventually used as the foundation for a trilogy of novels: Bounty Lands, Jonathan Blair: Bounty Lands Lawyer, and The Brooks Legend. Each of his novels appeared on best-seller lists, and the trilogy itself eventually earned its author a Pulitzer Prize nomination. The most important recurring theme in his works is the triumph of survival.

Exercises

Question 1. Duke is a Doberman. What are the other known breeds of dogs?

Answer Some known breeds of dogs are greyhound, dalmatian, alsatian, poodle, labrador, bull dog etc.

Question 2. Match the words in the boxes with their explanations given below

rampageous	subdural haemorrhage	bellow
blonde	taut	rambunctiousness
grin	critical	confinement
quivering	shimmied	

(a) This is the other word for trembling ______________

(b) This is used for smile______________

(c) You call a person this if he/she has pale gold coloured hair ___

(d) This is a quality which relates to high energy and noise_______

(e) This is related to dancing or moving in a way that involves shaking your hips and shoulders ________________

(f) This is to express a tendency to show violent and wild behaviour often causing damage ________________

(g) We use it for a condition which is serious, uncertain and dangerous ____________

(h) This is a state in which one is forced to stay in a closed space__

(i) This is a medical condition involving bleeding in the brain ____

(j) It is a loud, deep shout to show anger ____________________

(k) This is a condition when the rope or leash is stretched tightly__________________

Answer

(a) Quivering (b) Grin
(c) Blonde (d) Rambunctiousness
(e) Shimmied (f) Rampageous
(g) Critical (h) Confinement
(i) Subdural haemorrhage (j) Bellow
(k) Taut

Question 3. Based on your reading of the story answer the following questions by choosing the correct option.

(a) With reference to Hooper, the author says, "Everything was going for him". What does it imply?
   (i) He had everything that a man aspires for
   (ii) People admired him
   (iii) He did what he wanted
   (iv) He was capable of playing games

Answer (i) It means he had everything that a man aspires for.

(b) Duke never jumped on Chuck again because
   (i) Duke was paralysed and unable to jump
   (ii) Chuck was angry with Duke for jumping at him
   (iii) Duke realised that Chuck was not well and could not balance himself
   (iv) Marcy did not allow Duke to come near Chuck

Answer (iii) Duke realised that Chuck was not well and could not balance himself.

(c) The author says that Duke 'knew his job'. The job was
   (i) to look after Chuck
   (ii) to get Chuck on his feet
   (iii) to humour Chuck
   (iv) to guard the house

Answer (ii) The job was to get Chuck on his feet.

(d) '......even Duke's presence didn't reach Chuck". Why?

(i) Duke was locked in his kennel and Chuck couldn't see him

(ii) Duke hid himself behind the bed post

(iii) Duke had come to know that Hooper was not well

(iv) Hooper was lost in his own grief and pain

Answer (iv) '......even Duke's presence didn't reach Chuck', because Hooper was lost in his own grief and pain.

Question 4. Answer the following questions briefly.

(a) In 1953, Hooper was favoured young man. Explain.

Answer Hooper was favoured young man, means he was physically fit and mentally alert for official job. He was tall, strong and had a highly competitive nature. He was sound in sports and various other activities. Everything was good for him and his life was moving favourably smooth.

(b) They said that they would create a desk job for Hooper at headquarters.

(i) Who are 'they'?

Answer (i) 'They' were the top officials of Chuck's company.

(ii) Why did they decide to do this?

Answer They decided to do this because of Chuck's physical condition. As, left part of his body was paralysed after an accident and he could not move. properly. But Chuck was one of the most favoured young man of the office. The officials of his company wanted him to come out of his accident.

(c) Duke was an extraordinary dog. What special qualities did he exhibit to justify this? Discuss.

Answer When Duke met first time to Chuck after his accident, he understood his physical condition. Being a dog, Duke made his master walk regularly which enabled Chuck to move. Duke acted like a nurse and guide for Chuck who helped him to move daily. Chuck's neighbours and Marcy were the witnesses of Duke's extraordinary qualities.

(d) What problems did Chuck present when he returned to the company headquarters?

Answer In Chuck's company, nobody believed that he could handle his job. Nothing could be done to the salesman, who could not move around and worked for one hour only, each day. However, Hooper proved everybody wrong.

(e) Why do you think Charles Hooper's appointment as Assistant National Sales Manager is considered to be a tribute to Duke?

Answer Duke made Hooper stand on his legs and move again after helped him to the accident. Duke saved Hooper from going into depression and helped him to recover soon. This was a great service by a dog to his master. This service only enabled Chuck to join his office back. Therefore, Chuck's promotion can be considered as a tribute to Duke.

Question 5. Following dates were important in Charles Hooper's life in some way. Complete the table by relating the description with the correct dates.

January 4, March 1, June 1, October 12

Date	Description
(a)	News spread that Hooper and Duke had made it to an intersection.
(b)	Hooper walked independently from the clinic to the branch office.
(c)	Hooper planned to start a full day's work at office.
(d)	Duke met with a fatal accident.

Answer

(a) June 1
(b) January 4
(c) March 1
(d) October 12

Question 6. Given below are five qualities that Charles Hooper displayed during his struggle.

courage | perseverance | determination | endurance | faith

Get into groups of five. Each team will choose one quality to talk about to the whole class for about one minute. But before you talk you have two minutes to think about it. You can make notes if you wish.

Answer

Group 1 I would say that Charles Hooper displayed some rare qualities of head and heart. He was taken to the hospital in a severe condition. He was unable to talk, he could only breathe and see. After six weeks of the accident he was put on a wheel chair. He struggled and survived. He did not give up. It is his courage that made everybody surprised.

Group 2 Hooper also showed perseverance in what he started to do for survival. Though, he was in great pain. and couldn't move his left side, but with Duke's help he struggled hard. He asked Marcy to help him to his feet. He set a goal for himself and tried hard to achieve it. It was his perseverance that made him fit.

Group 3 Hooper showed determination. Hooper had become a victim of boredom, but Duke didnot want his master to lie bored. He was determined to make his master walk. Duke proved a charger of a battery. In the beginning Hooper walked one step. Due to his determination these steps began to increases and finally Hooper was able to walk full time.

Group 4 Hooper showed plenty of endurance. The dog had faith in himself that he would be successful in making his master walk. Hooper also had a great faith and determination Self-confidence made Hooper an example of a fighting spirit. He hit the target of walking due to his endurance.

Groups 5 Hooper's ultimate victory over his paralytic state showed his faith in himself. He realised that with the help of Duke, He could overcome his incapability. He had a great faith and determination. After the accident, his faith in himself lay dormant. But Duke's coming from the Kennel proved a blessing for Hooper. Duke ignited the flame of determination in Hooper's mind. With the strong determination and faith in himself Hooper became fit for his official duty.

Listening Task

Question 7. Listen to an excerpt from a news telecast on a national channel carefully and complete the table given below.

Brave Hearts

S.N.	Name of the Brave-Heart	Place They Belong to	Reason for Award
1.	Saumik Mishra	Uttar Pradesh	foiled theft
2.	Prachi Santosh Sen		saved a child
3.	Kavita Kanwar	Chhattisgarh	
4.		Jodhpur	dodged marriage to 40 year old
5.	Rahul Balloon Seller	Delhi/National Capital	
6.	M Marudu Pandi	Tamil Nadu	averted rail disaster
7.		Bengaluru	saved a baby caught in bull fight
8.	Silver Kharbani	Meghalaya	
9.	Yumkhaibam Addison Singh		saved an eight year old from drowning
10		Uttar Pradesh	saved people from drowning
11.		Haryana/Jind	helped nab armed miscreants
12.	Kritika Jhanwar		fought off robbers

Answer

S.N.	Name of the Brave-Heart	Place They Belong to	Reason for Award
1.	Saumik Mishra	Uttar Pradesh	Failed theft
2.	Prachi Santosh Sen	Madhya Pradesh	Saved a child
3.	Kavita Kanwar	Chhattisgarh	Saved three inmates caught in a kitchen fire
4.	Kanwar	Jodhpur	Dodged marriage to 40 year old
5.	Rahul balloon seller	Delhi/National Capital	Identified the man who planted bombs
6.	M Marudu Pandi	Tamil Nadu	Averted rail disaster
7.	Gagan and Bhoomika J Murthy	Bengaluru	Saved a baby caught in bull fight
8.	Silver Kharbani	Meghalaya	Saved the life of her cousin trapped in fire
9.	Yumkhaibam Addison Singh	Manipur	Saved an eight year old from drowning
10	Shahan Shah	Uttar Pradesh	Saved people from drowning
11.	Manish Bansal	Haryana/Jind	Helped nab armed miscreants
12.	Kritika Thanwar	Rajasthan	Fought off robbers

Writing Task

Question 8. Read the diary entry written by Charles Hooper on the day he received the order,"......Charles Hooper is appointed Assistant National Sales Manager."

March 1, 19.... Thursday 10 pm

Last four years have been eventful. The day I brought Duke home.... (Marcy was almost impolite to him because she would have preferred a Pomeranian to a Doberman) .... to a stage on October 12, 1957 (when she would not allow anyone else to carry the injured Duke to the vet)... much water has flowed under the bridge.

From being a very fit high-charging zone sales manager, I was reduced to a paralysed cripple forced to lie on a bed alone with my thoughts due to a small error by a car driver. Despair had led me on to helplessness... Was I to be a vegetable for the rest of my life? I never wanted to be a burden on Marcy.

Duke's re-entry into my life lifted my numb spirits. The day he made me take my first step, there was a rekindled hope. Duke assumed all the responsibility for leading me back to my office desk ... Life had taken a full circle. From shock to denial and helplessness to anger, Duke taught me to cope with the challenge and led me to accept the changed mode of life. I am happy to be living as well as working successfully.

The order that I have received today is my tribute to Duke who would always be alive with me and be a part of everything else I achieve in my life.

When a person loses something, he is shocked and gets into a state of denial leading to anger. In such a situation, coping well leads to acceptance and a changed way of living in view of the loss. Taking cues from what happened or might have happened with Hooper, write your views in the form of an article about 'Coping with Loss' in 150-175 words.

Answer Our life is a blend of happiness and sorrow. Rather we can say these are the two sides of the same coin. Life is not a bed of roses. But life has good things after every bad ones. When. Hopper met with the accident which paralysed him, he felt every depressed. But his dog, Duke's re-entry into his life rekindled hope in him.

Duke taught him to cope with the challenge and Hooper accepted it. Even a doctor could not do whatever Duke did for him. Duke encouraged his master to walk more and more. This support helped Hooper to achieve his goal. He proved that God helps those who help themselves.

The story of Hooper's struggle is very inspiring. He displayed a strong wlll power to overcome his physical disability. He fought with his courage and determination. Finally, he rose to be at the top of his career. Hooper rediscoved the meaning of life by discarding all his losses.

Poetry

1

The Brook

Alfred Lord Tennyson

Synopsis

'The Brook' is a poem written by 'Lord Alfred Tennyson'. In this poem, the Brook itself is the narrator where it describes its experiences as it flows towards the brimming river, an ultimate destination. Poet has personified the Brook. He has equated the life of the Brook with the human life. The poet has metaphorically compared the man and the nature. This poem reveals that the life of a man is short and limited but the nature is eternal.

Detailed Summary

The Brook's Origin

The Brook narrates the story of its origin. It says that it comes out from the places, which are frequently visited by the water birds like coots and herns. It emerges suddenly and then flows down to the valley with a lot of noise.

Journey of the Brook

The Brook moves hurriedly down the hills and slips down the ridges. It moves through a small village and under about fifty bridges. It then flows down the Phillips farm and finally falls in the brimming river. The poet compares it to the human life by saying, human life ends whereas a Brook flows for hundreds of years.

When it flows through stony ways and more into spirals it creates different and a lot of noise. It talks to itself while moving. It gets angry, It passes the curves of its banks and passes through the fallow fields, fairy foreland and many other places. These are covered with willow weeds and plants like mallow. Then finally, it joins the brimming river.

It carries many fish along with it like lusty trout, and grayling flowers and leaves sails over its surface and foamy flakes can also be seen over it. Water is clear, and the surface of the river shines in the Sun beam. It carries everything along with it to the brimming river.

As the Brook enters in the lawns and grassy plots, it flows with less speed. It moves from the sides of hazel trees and carries sweet flowers called forget-me-not with it. These flowers are grown for happy and young lovers. Swallow flies and the Sunrays dance over its surface.

It makes soft noise during night when it passes through the thorny routes. It moves through the curves made of pebbles in the way and then finally joins the brimming river, the ultimate destination.

About the Poet

Lord Tennyson was born in year 1809 and died in 1892. He was born in Lincolnshire. He was an author of victorian era of literature. He wrote many short poems and retained a large audience for his poetry. His poetry had perfect control over synthesis of sound and meaning, and the union of pictorial and musical theme.

After Wordsworth's death in 1850, Tennyson was appointed to the position of poet Laureate, which he held until his death in 1892.

Exercises

Question 1. Can you match the following?

(a) Something that lives for one year	biennial
(b) Something that lives for about two years	perennial
(c) Something that lives for more than two years	annual

Answer (a) annual, (b) biennial, (c) perennial

Question 2. Here is a list of few things. Can you tell how long each of them can live/exist?

(a) A dog
(b) An elephant
(c) A tree
(d) A human being
(e) A star
(f) A mountain
(g) A river

Answer (a) 10 to 13 years (b) 50 to 70 years
(c) 300 years (d) 100 years
(e) Indefinite period (f) Indefinite period
(g) Indefinite period

Question 3. The poem is about a Brook. A dictionary would define a Brook as a stream or a small river. Read the poem silently first. After the first reading, the teacher will make you listen to a recording of the poem. What do you think the poem is all about?

Answer The poem is about the life of a Brook. The Brook is personified. The journey of the brook is different from that of human journey. The journey of the Brook is continuous whereas the journey of human comes to an end. The Brook is immortal whereas man is mortal.

Question 4. After reading the poem, answer the following questions.
The poet has used a number of words which indicate 'movement' and 'sound'. Working with your partner, make a list of these words from the poem and complete the web chart.

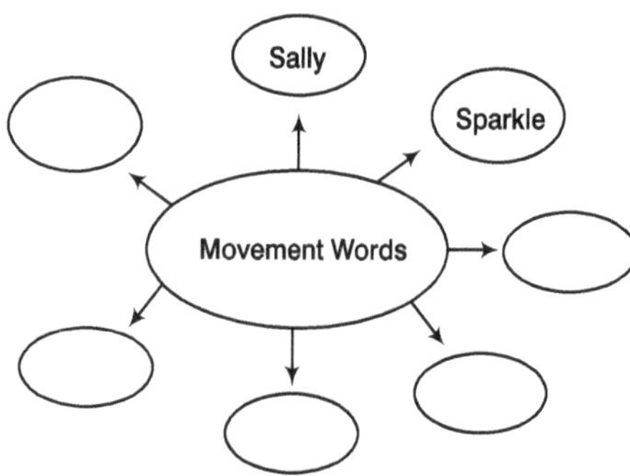

Answer

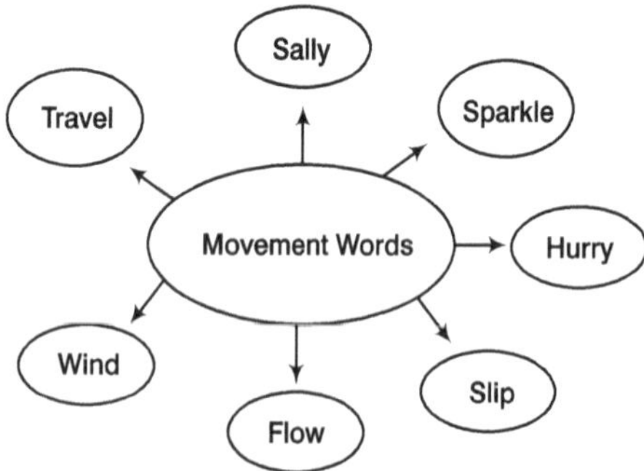

(b)

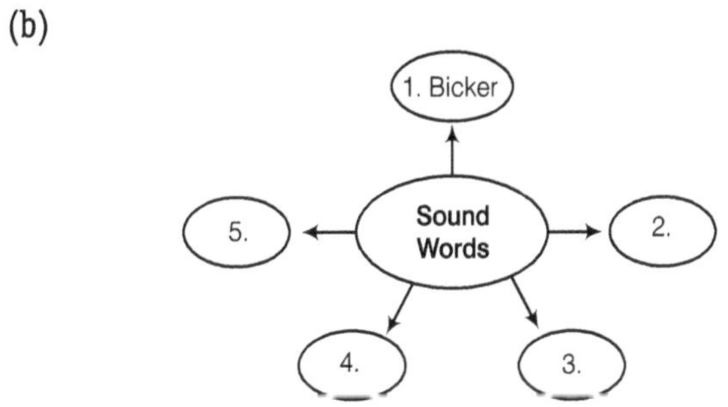

Answer

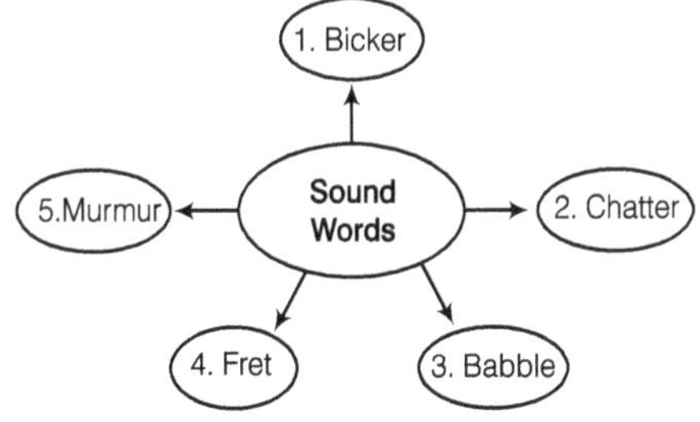

(c) A word or a combination of words, whose sound seems to resemble the sound it denotes (*e.q.*, 'hiss', 'buzz' etc) is called onomatopoeia. From the words that you have filled in the blurbs above point out these words.

Answer The onomatopoeia words are chatter babble, fret, murmur.

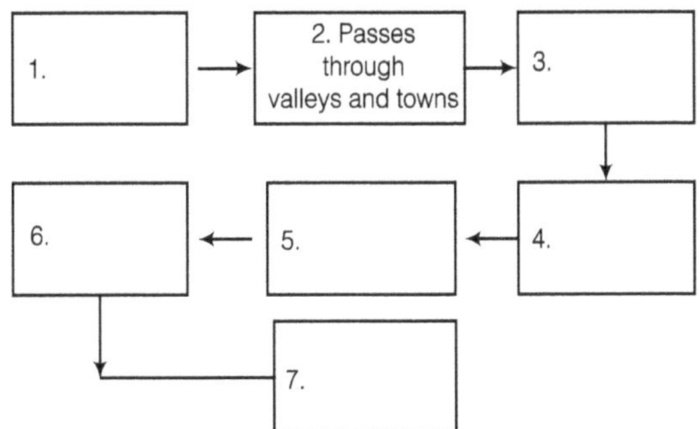

The following is a flow chart showing the course of the brook. Can you fill in the blank spaces with help from phrases given below?

(a) Passes under fifty bridges
(b) Comes from the place where coots and herons live
(c) Passes lawns filled with flowers

(d) Crosses both fertile and fallow land
(e) Goes through wilderness full of thorny bushes

Answer

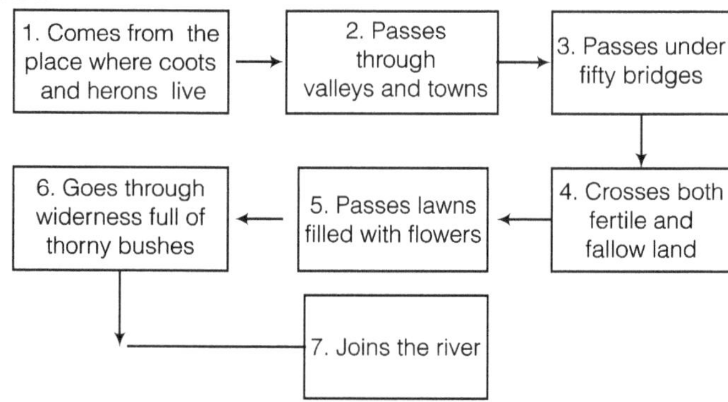

Question 5. On the basis of your understanding of the poem, answer the following questions by ticking the correct choice.

(a) The message of the poem is that the life of a brook is
(i) temporary (ii) short lived
(iii) eternal (iv) momentary
Answer (iii)

(b) The poet draws a parallelism between the journey of the brook with
(i) the life of a man
(ii) the death of man
(iii) the difficulties in a man's life
(iv) the endless talking of human beings
Answer (i)

(c) The poem is narrated in the first person by the brook. This figure of speech is
(i) Personification
(ii) Metaphor
(iii) Simile
(iv) Transferred epithet
Answer (i)

(d) In the poem, below mentioned lines
"And here and there a lusty trout,
And here and there a grayling"
suggest that.........

(i) the brook is a source of life
(ii) people enjoy the brook
(iii) fishes survive because of water
(iv) the brook witnesses all kinds of scenes

Answer (iii)

Question 6. Answer the following questions

(a) How does the brook 'sparkle'?

Answer When the Sun rays fall on the emerging the brook, it sparkles. To personify the brook, the word 'sparkle' has been used by the poet.

(b) 'Bicker' means 'to quarrel'. Why does the poet use this word here?

Answer 'Bicker' here means to move down hurriedly with lot of noise towards valley. The Brook makes a lot of noise when it flows down. The poet uses this word to describe that inmaking lot of noise the brook seems to be quarrelling.

(c) How many hills and bridges does the brook pass during its journey?

Answer The brook passes down the thirty hills and flows around under fifty bridges. It moves with its full speed and makes lot of noise.

(d) Where does it finally meet the river?

Answer After crossing various bridges, ridges, hills, towns and villages, the brook reaches to the Phillip's farm. Phillip's farm is situated near the brimming river. From Phillip's farm it joins the brimming river.

(e) Why does the word 'chatter' repeated in the poem?

Answer The word 'chatter' is repeated to show the continuous movement and noise made by the brook. It also provides flow and rhythm to the poem.

(f) 'With many a curve my banks I fret'. What does the poet mean by the statement?

Answer The poet shows by this statement that the water hits forcefully at the curves on the banks of the brook. It looks as if the brook is angry with the curves of the banks.

(g) "I wind about, and in and out". What kind of picture does this line create in your mind?

Answer It creates a picture of water flowing freely in a zig-zag manner.

(h) Name the different things that can be found floating in the brook.

Answer Different things move along with the water of the brook. Blossoms sail on its surface, fishes like trout and grayling live in it, foamy flakes flow over its surface and sweet forget-me-not flowers flow in it.

(i) What does poet want to convey by using the words 'steal' and 'slide'?

Answer The poet wants to convey that the brook, quietly passes through the hurdles and it is slipping through some obstruction in its flow. Sandy banks, trees, wild growth etc are the obstructions in the way of the brook.

(j) The poem has many examples of alliteration. List any five examples.

Answer Examples of alliteration are

(i) 'I slip, I slide, I gloom, I glance'

(ii) 'Skimming swallows'

(iii) 'With willow-weed'

(iv) 'I babble on the pebbles'

(v) 'Fairy foreland set'

(k) 'I make the netted sunbeam dance'. What does netted sunbeam' mean? How does it dance?

Answer When the reflection of Sun rays fall on the surface of slowly moving water of the brook, it gleams and seems dancing as the water flows.

(l) What is the 'refrain' in the poem? What effect does it create?

Answer The 'refrain' in the poem is

"For men may come and men may go,

But I go on forever".

It gives the central idea of the poem and creates the permanence of the central theme throughout the poem. It also tell us the permanent aspect of the brook and the temporary aspect of human life.

Question 7. Read the given lines and answer the questions.

I chatter, chatter, as I flow
To join the brimming river,
For men may come and men may go,
But I go on forever.

(a) What does 'I' refer to in the given lines?

Answer 'I' refers to the brook.

(b) How does it chatter?

Answer It 'chatters' when its water flows over the stony bed.

(c) Why was the poet used the word 'brimming'? What kind of a picture does it create?

Answer The poet has used the word 'brimming' with the river to show that life is full of joys like the river is full of water up to its brims.

(d) Explain the last two lines of the stanza.

Answer The last two lines mean that human beings are mortal, they do not live forever, but the brook is eternal, it goes on forever.

Question 8. Identify the rhyme scheme of the poem.

Answer The rhyme scheme of the poem is ab, ab, cd, cd, ef, ef, and so on.

Question 9. The poem is full of images that come alive through skillful use of words. List out any two images that appeal to you the most, quoting the lines from the poem.

Answer The brook emerges or takes birth and comes down the valley suddenly. The poet has described the incident in a pictorial form. The image of water coming out suddenly, water birds flying around and water moving down the valley making loud noise is defined in the first stanza.

Second image is of zig-zag movement of the water. It moves carrying on its surface many blossoms and leaves. Fresh water fish like 'trout' and 'grayling' can be seen gliding at its bottom.

Question 10. The brook appears to be a symbol for life. Pick out examples of parallelism between life and the brook.

Answer The examples of parallelism in the poem are

(i) **Young Age** When one is young, he is strong and full of enthusiasm. Similarly, the brook in its youth hurries down. It makes huge noise and rushes forcefully towards its destination. It 'sallies', 'bickers' and 'chatters' while it flows.

(ii) **Supports** Human beings are a source of support of life for each other by providing help to each other, in the same way the brook also supports life of fishes like 'trout' and 'grayling'. So, both men and the Brook are similar.

(iii) **Old Age** In old age, man become calm, and wise. In the same way, the brook also slows down and starts moving slowly towards its destination. Men dies and the brook joins the brimming river.

2

The Road Not Taken

Robert Frost

Synopsis

The road in the poem is the metaphor for life. The poem suggests that we all have to take decisions in our life. Our decisions depend on our character, our thinking and our decision-making ability. Once, we have taken a decision, there is no return.

Detailed Summary

The Poet at a Fork

Once a poet was standing in a forest at the time of autumn. The point where the poet was standing had two roads diverging into the different directions. The poet tried to analyse the better path by looking as far as he could. He could see upto a point where it turned to the undergrowth.

The Poet's Decision

One of the roads looked easier to travel as many people had travelled through it. Whereas another road was too grassy and looked as if less number of travellers had passed through it. The poet decided to adopt the second road.

However, at first the poet was not sure about his decision. He said that morning falls on both the roads equally, but still nobody stepped on this road. He was the first one for the day to move on that road. Therefore, he doubted whether he should continue or not.

In the last stanza, the poet decided to move forward. He thought that after ages he would tell one fact of life with a sigh. It was that, between two roads, he selected one road, which was less travelled by others. And this particular decision in life made all the difference in his life. It is an eternal truth and can be applicable to all human beings.

About the Poet

Robert Frost was born in the year 1874 at San Franscisco and died in the year 1963. American editors rejected his poetry. Frost then moved to England alongwith his family in 1912 and a London publisher published his book in the same year. Later on Frost achieved his reputation in his own country also. He became one of America's best loved poets. Frost choose to follow traditional patterns in his poems. Despite the surface cheerfulness and descriptive accuracy of his poems, he often presents a dark, sober vision of life and there is a decidedly thoughtful quality to his work.

Exercises

Question 1. Sometimes the choices we make have far-reaching consequences. Think about choices you make on a daily basis and the importance of these choices.

Answer Answer to this question may vary from student to student as the question involves personal likes and dislikes. *e.g.*,

Choices	Result
Eating dosa, chaat	Indigestion and extra calories
or	
Food made at home	More tasty, good for health
Reading thoroughly all the reference books	Clear concepts about subject matter and getting good marks
or	
Reading only notes given by the coaching center	Incomplete knowledge and getting mediocre marks

Question 2. Complete the web chart showing choices and decisions you may have to make in the next few years and the factors that affect these choices.

Determining Factors

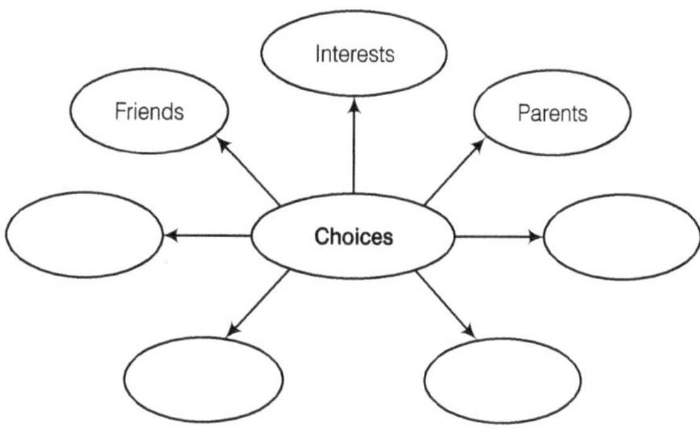

Answer

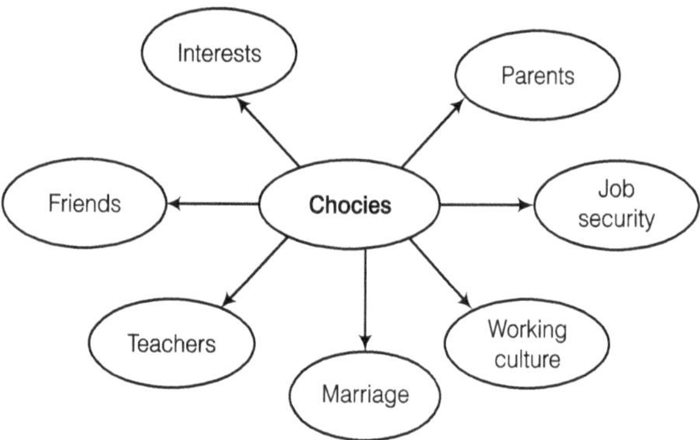

This is a very subjective and it varies from student to student.

Question 3. Have you made choices that are acceptable and less 'risky' or have you followed the beaten track? Why?

Answer I would choose a less risky path in life, as risky path may drop one into uncertainties and downfall and I don't want to face insecurity and disappointment in my life.

Question 4. List common dilemmas that teenagers face involving the choice of one or more 'roads'. Give examples of 'roads' that you must travel, (*e.g.*, facing peer pressure, choosing friends, observing rules laid down by school and parents, acting on your own values.)

Answer The dilemmas could be

(i) Choosing between the streams (humanities, commerce, science etc.)
(ii) Choosing of different professions
(iii) Choosing schools/colleges for higher education
(iv) Chooaing one's atyle clothing

Question 5. Answer the following questions

(a) What choice did the poet have to make?

Answer The poet had to select one road between the two. He faced a dilemma. He stood there for long and then he decide to choose that road which seemed led to be less travelled. He felt it would make all the difference to his future life.

(b) Did he regret his choice? Why/Why not?

Answer The poet regretted his choice because the leftout road seemed to be equally less travelled. He could not take both the roads at the same time. He kept the first road 'reserved' for some other day. The road, he selected was the cause of all the differences in his life. His utterings revealed his regret.

Question 6. On the basis of your understanding of the poem, answer the following questions by ticking the correct choice.

(a) In the poem, a traveller comes to a fork in the road and needs to decide which way to go, to continue his journey. Figuratively the choice of the road denotes

(i) the tough choices people make the road of life
(ii) the time wasted on deciding what to do
(iii) life is like a forest
(iv) one most travel a lot to realise his dreams

Answer (i)

(b) The poet writes, 'Two roads diverged' in a yellow wood. The word diverged means

(i) appeared
(ii) curved
(iii) branched off
(iv) continued on

Answer (ii)

(c) The tone of the speaker in the first stanza is that of

(i) excitement

(ii) anger

(iii) hesitation and thoughtfulness

(iv) sorrow

Answer (iii)

Question 7. Answer the following questions briefly.

(i) Describe the two roads that the author comes across.

Answer The two roads that the author comes across are

(a) First, which was frequently travelled by the people. It symbolised a common and easier path in life which most of the people decide to undertake.

(b) Second, which was not frequently travelled by the people. It symbolised the path which was difficult and people generally decide to leave it in their lives.

(ii) Which road does speaker choose and why?

Answer Speaker selected the road which was less travelled by the people because he wanted to create a difference and exploring new avenues in life.

(iii) Does the speaker seem happy about his decision?

Answer The speaker was not happy about his decision. After some time he regretted to take the second road which was uncommon and difficult to travel on. He believed that his choice made all the difference in his life. This showed his hesitation and unhappiness. But he knew the reality that life could not give us ultimate contentment.

(iv) The poet says, "I took one less travelled by And that has made all the difference". What is 'the difference' that the poet mentions?

Answer The poet mentioned the difference in success by his decision. He regretted for his own decision. In life we can not start everything again, instead of going ahead. Whatever decision we take in our life decides about the success and achievement in our lives.

Question 8. What is the rhyme scheme of the poem?

Answer The rhyme scheme of the poem is a b a a b.

Question 9. Fill in the blanks to complete the following paragraph that gives the theme of the poem. Use the words given in the box below.

decision, sorry, foresee, choices, pleasant, direction, fork, trail, rewarding, chance, wonder, both

The poem "The Road Not Taken" by Robert Frost is about the _______ that one makes in life. It tells about a man who comes to a _______ in the road he is travelling upon. He feels _______ that he can not travel _______ paths as he must choose one. Frost uses this fork in the road to represent a point in the man's life where he has to choose the _______ he wishes to take in life. As he thinks about his ______ he looks down one path as far as he can see trying to _______ what life will be like if he walks that path. He then gazes at the other and decides the outcome of going down that path would be just as ______ . At this point, he concludes that the _______ that has been less travelled on would be more _______ when he reaches the end of it. The man then decides that he will save the other path for another day, even though he knows that one path leads to another and that he won't get a _______ to go back. The man then says that he will be telling this story with a sigh someday in the future suggesting that he will _______ what life would have been like if he had chosen the more walked path even though the path he chose has made all the difference.

Answer choices, fork, sorry, both, direction, decision, foresee, rewarding, trail, pleasant, chance, wonder.

Question 10. Roads are fascinating as metaphors for life, change, journeys, partings, adventure, etc or simply as roads. This is probably why they and all their attendant images, have permeated art, literature and song. In the poem, Frost uses the fork in the road as a metaphor for the choices we make in life. Thus, the roads are, in fact, two alternative ways of life. What other nouns could be used to represent life?

- River
- _______
- _______
- _______

Answer
- River
- Flower
- Modes of transport
- Rain

Question 11. 'The Road Not Taken' is a biographical poem. Therefore, some personal biographical information is relevant to the deeper understanding of the poem we have read. Go to www.encarta.com and complete the following worksheet about Robert Frost.

(a) What "momentous decisions" was made by Frost in 1912?

Answer The momentous decision was to move to England with family.

(b) How old was he when took his decision?

Answer He was thirty eight years old when he took this decision.

(c) Why was it so difficult to make his decision? Think and give more than one reason.

Answer Frost took a difficult decision of leaving USA. He sold his farm and it was not so easy. He did not earn fame as a good poet in USA. Even he was not sure about his future in England still he took a difficult decision to migrate to England.

(d) Was the "road" Frost had taken easy "to travel"?

Answer The road Frost had taken was not easy to travel. It was risky to move from native place. It was difficult to establish and prove his merit in an alien place.

(e) Do you think he wrote "The Road Not Taken" before sailing from the USA to England or after? Can you quote a line or two from the poem that can support your answer?

Answer I think Frost wrote 'The Road Not Taken' after sailing from the USA to England. Lines from the poem that can support my view point are

Two roads diverged in a wood ....

I took the one less travelled by

And that has made all the difference.

(f) Do you think Frost finally became popular in America as a poet?

Answer Yes, his success in England finally made him popular in America as a poet. In 1950, the US Senate felicitated Frost in his 75th birthday for being a popular poet.

3

The Solitary Reaper

William Wordsworth

Synopsis

While travelling through Scotland, the poet heard a solitary reaper singing a folk song. The song was so melodious that he stood mesmerised and heard it silently. However, the poet could not understand the theme or language of the song, yet the song remained resounding in his ears.

Detailed Summary

Poet Sees the Reaper

While passing through the highlands of Scotland, the poet saw a lonely Scottish girl singing in the field. She was singing alone and working there. She was cutting the crops and binding the grains. The song was sad. The poet stood silently there and listened to her song. The whole deep valley was filled with her sound. The poet did not move or make any noise for fear that she would stop singing.

The Sweetness of the Reaper's Song

The poet compared the song of the girl with the nightingale's song. The nightingale sings very sweetly in the deserts of Arabia to travellers. The singing comforts them when they are tired. The poet felt that no nightingale could have sung as sweetly as the solitary reaper sang.

The poet found the song of the solitary reaper sweeter than the song of the cuckoo bird. Cuckoo birds welcome the weary sailors. Their songs comfort them. Their songs break the silence of the sea during spring season.

Mystery About the Song

The solitary reaper has a selfish air. The poet could not understand her song as she was singing in her mother tongue.

The poet is curious to know the theme of the song. The poet said that perhaps the girl was singing a sad song for something unhappy which happened in the past. It might be due to a loss in some battle. The poet guessed that she might be singing some ordinary song for problems in day-to-day life.

The poet further guessed that the song could be for some natural sorrow, loss, pain, disaster etc. that happened in the past and could happen in future also.

The Song's Effect on the Poet

Lastly, the poet said that whatever was the theme of the song, it locked in his heart. The girl was singing endlessly. She was singing while she was working with her sickle in the field.

The poet could not move and he heard the melodious song of the girl standing motionless and still. While mounting up the hill, the music was deeply engraved in the heart of the poet even when he could not hear it anymore.

About the Poet

William Wordsworth was born in Cockermouth in the Lake District, England on 7th April, 1770. Wordsworth was the poet for the common man who wrote in ordinary language to express his feelings on nature, children, the poor and common people. He said, "Poetry is the spontaneous overflow of powerful feelings" arising from "emotions recollected in tranquility". He died on 23rd April, 1850.

Exercises

Question 1. Sometimes we see something beautiful and striking and we remember it for a long time afterwards. Can you recollect this ever happening to you? If so, what was it? What do you remember about it now? Are the details of what you saw or the feelings you experienced at that time fresh in your mind? Think for a few minutes, then share your thoughts with the class.

Answer I am very fond of flowers. I remember when I visited 'mughal garden' for the first time with my parents, the pleasant breeze made the place lovely. The Mughal Gardens are situated at the back of the Rashtrapati Bhavan. Main garden - Two channels running North to South and two running East to West divide the garden into a grit of squares. There are six lotus shaped fountains at the crossing of these channels. Enclosed in walls about twelve feet high this is predominantly a rose garden. It has16 square rose beds encased in low hedger. I thought I have entered a heaven. The grassy lawns added its beauty. The vast variety of flowers were blooming. The garden contains several varieties of rose, marigold, bougainvillea, sweet william etc. The atmosphere of the garden is superb and magical. Its beauty is still fresh in my heart.

Question 2. The poet could not understand the words of the song, yet he raised several possibilities about its theme. In the diagram below are some of these possibilities. Read the third stanza again and find the phrase that matches each. Copy and complete the diagram, writing each phrase in the empty boxes. Work in pairs.

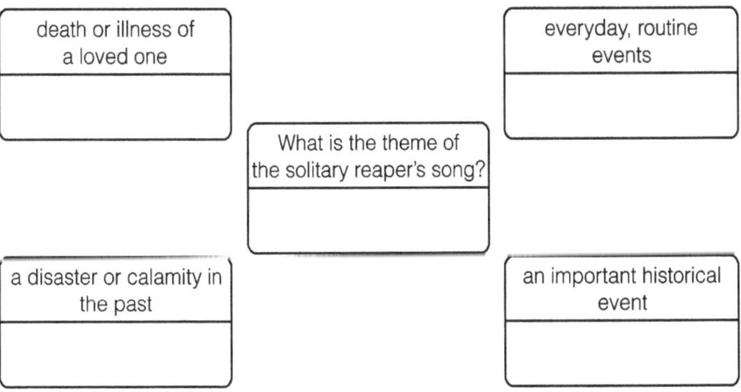

Answer

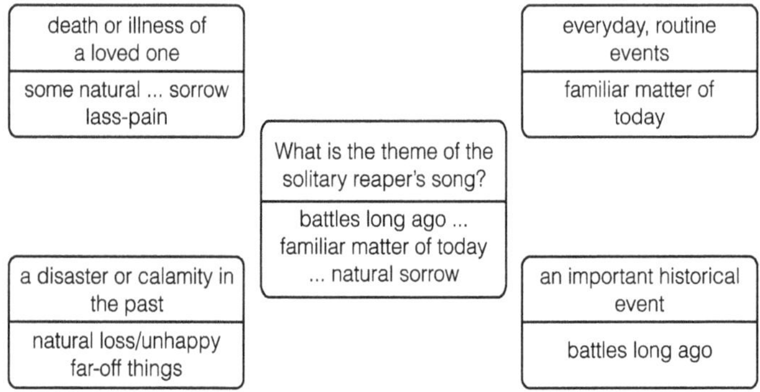

Question 3. On the basis of your understanding of the poem, answer the following questions by ticking the correct choice.

(a) The central idea of the poem 'The Solitary Reaper' is
- (i) well sung songs give us happiness
- (ii) melodious sounds appeal to all
- (iii) beautiful experiences give us life long pleasure
- (iv) reapers can sing like birds

Answer (iii)

(b) In the poem 'The Solitary Reaper' to whom does the poet say 'Stop here or gently pass'?
- (i) To the people cutting corn
- (ii) To himself
- (iii) To the people who make noise
- (iv) To all the passers by

Answer (iv)

(c) 'The Solitary Reaper' is a narrative poem set to music. This form of verse is called a
- (i) ballad
- (ii) soliloquy
- (iii) monologue
- (iv) sonnet

Answer (i)

(d) The poet's lament in the poem 'The Solitary Reaper' is that
- (i) he cannot understand the song
- (ii) he did not know the lass
- (iii) she stopped singing at once
- (iv) he had to move away

Answer (iv)

(e) The setting of the poem is

(i) Arabia (ii) Hebrides

(iii) Scotland (iv) England

Answer (iii)

Question 4. (a) Read the second stanza again, in which Wordsworth compares the Solitary Reaper's song with the song of the nightingale and the cuckoo. On the basis of your reading (and your imagination), copy and complete the table below.

	Place	Heard by	Impact on Listener
Solitary Reaper	Scottish Highlands	the poet	holds him spellbound
Nightingale			
Cuckoo			

Answer

	Place	Heard by	Impact on Listener
Solitary Reaper	Scottish highlands	the poet	holds him spellbound
Nightingale	Arabian Desert, oasis	tired travellers	travellers feel fresh
Cuckoo	Farthest Island Hebrides	sailors	breaks the silence

(b) Why do you think Wordsworth has chosen the song of the nightingale and the cuckoo, for comparison with Solitary Reaper's song?

Answer William Wordsworth has chosen the songs of the nightingale and the cuckoo bird for comparison to describe the sweetness, melody and freshness of the song of the solitary reaper. By this comparison, the poet created an effect on the reader that the song of the solitary reaper was extra-ordinary melodious and refreshing. Even the poet wanted to say that her song was sweeter than the songs of a nightingale and a cuckoo.

(c) As you read the second stanza, what pictures come to your mind? Be ready to describe them in your own words, to the rest of the class.

Answer The second stanza makes us visualise two pictures in our mind. The first is the picture of nightingale entertaining weary travellers in some shady haunt among Arabian Desert. The second picture is of cuckoo bird singing sweetly to reveal the coming of the spring break and their songs the silence of the sea.

Question 5. In the sixth line of the first stanza, we read

" .... and sings a melancholy strain ....".

This "s" sound at the beginning of sings and strain has been repeated. Poets often do this. Do you know why? Do you know what this "poetic repetition" is called? Can you find other instances of this, in 'The Solitary Reaper'?

Answer This poetic repetition is called 'alliteration'. The poet often use this poetic device to give musical touch to their creations.

The other instances are

(i) Repetition of 'l' sound in - Yon solitary Highland Lass.

(ii) Repetition of 'S' sound in - Alone she cuts and binds the grain.

(iii) Repetition of 'l' sound in - Listened, motionless and still.

Question 6. In the first stanza, some words or phrases have been used to show that the girl working in fields is alone. Which are those words and phrases? What effect do they create in the mind of the reader?

Answer The words and phrases are

(i) 'Single in the field'.

(ii) 'You solitary highland lass'.

(iii) 'Reaping and singing by herself'.

These words and phrases create an effect of mystery and beauty. While the poet looks at the girl singing the song, the entire scene is very beautiful. As she is alone and busy in her work it comes with a mystery.

1

Drama

Villa For Sale

Sacha Guitry

Synopsis

'Villa for Sale' is a play written by 'Sacha Guitry' which dramatises the sale deal of a Villa. Juliette, the owner of the Villa has put it on sale but is unable to sell it. She wants to sell it as early as possible. Gaston and his wife Jeanne come to inspect it. Gaston is not willing to buy it. Jeanne goes upstairs with Juliette to inspect it. Gaston stays downstairs. Meanwhile, Mrs Al Smith comes. She is in a hurry. She buys the Villa in three hundred thousand francs from Gaston thinking him as the owner of the house. She pays the money by cheque. Juliette and Jeanne come down. Gaston buys the villa from Juliette in two hundred thousands francs and makes a clean profit of a hundred thousand francs. He takes the painting signed by Carot as a souvenir.

Detailed Summary

Juliette Wants to Sell her Villa

Juliette is sad that her Villa, which she wants to sell has not been yet sold. Nobody is ready to buy it and now she is ready to sacrifice it at any price. She is even ready to sell it at one hundred thousand francs though it cost her two hundred thousand francs. She is amazed that Villa has not been sold even when it is near to Joinville, the French Hollywood.

Gaston and his Wife Visit the Villa

Gaston and his wife Jeanne enter to inspect the Villa. Gaston is not willing to buy the Villa, whereas Jeanne wants it for her parents. Juliette explains all the benefits and facilities of the Villa and charges two hundred and fifty thousand francs for it. Later, she brings down the price to two hundred thousand francs. Juliette takes Jeanne upstairs to show bathrooms. Gaston is left alone.

Mrs Al Smith Makes a Deal

Meanwhile, Mrs Al Smith enters. She praises the Villa and thinks that Gaston is the owner of the house. She is a proud American actress and ready to buy it at any cost. She asks Gaston, why the price is not written on the board 'Villa for Sale'. She is in hurry and wants to buy the Villa in five minutes. She is not interested in any details of Villa as she wants to build a bungalow there. Gaston sells the Villa to Mrs Al Smith in three hundred thousand francs. Mrs Al Smith hurriedly signs the cheque and leaves saying that other formalities will be done by her lawyer, Mr Who.

Gaston Earns Profit

After Mrs Al Smith leaves, Juliette and Jeanne come down. Now, Gaston is ready to buy the Villa from Juliette in two hundred thousand francs. He signs the cheque and gives it to Juliette. He requests Juliette to let him take the picture signed by Carot as a souvenir. When Jeanne asks him what he has done, Gaston replies that he has made a profit of a hundred thousand francs. He also askes that he will tell her everything later.

About the Author

Sacha Guitry was born in Saint Petersburg, Russia, in 1885. He was the son of well-known actor Lucien Guitry. He was a French stage actor, film actor, director, screen writer and playwright. He wrote 12 plays, more than 30 books and direct 33 movies. He claimed that he staged a 'one-man revolt, against the dismal French theatre of his time. He was equally successful on screen and stage. He also earned recognition as a highly competent producer and direction. He died during the summer of 1957.

Exercises

Question 1. If you could buy your dream house today what are some specific features you would want for your house? Write them in the bubbles below.

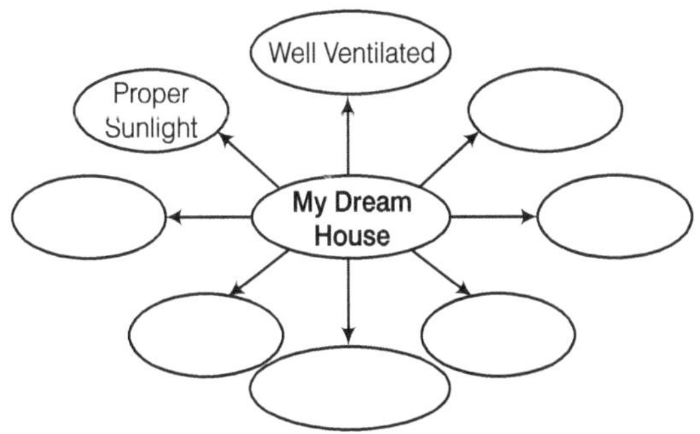

Answer

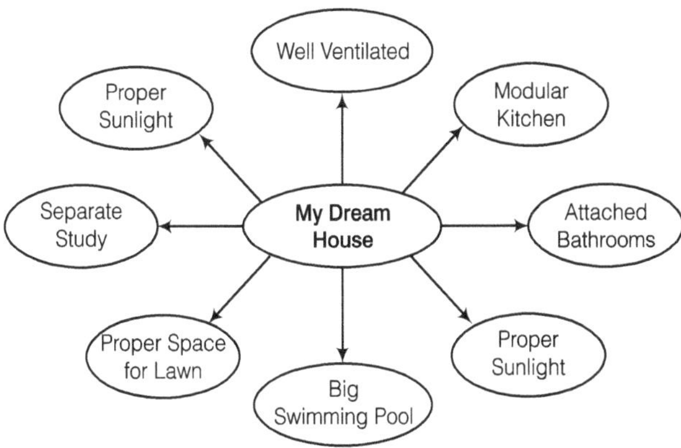

Question 2. Discuss with your partner the similarities and dissimilarities in your dream house.

Answer To be discussed in the class with a partner.

For example My dream was to have a bungalow with all latest facilities. I wanted a big lawn and a garden full of beautiful flowers. My bungalow should be in a posh colony. I also wanted a big swimming pool where I can enjoy myself in summers. The difference was that my friend was looking for a disco party hall in the house but I don't prefer it.

Question 3. Copy and complete the following paragraph about the theme of the play using the clues given in the box below. Remember that there are more clues than required.

sell, buying, house, enthusiastic, comes 200 thousand francs, taking, favour, get, sleeps, money, 250 thousand francs, unhappy, his in-laws, walks in, strikes, keep

Juliette, the owner of a Villa wants to __(I)____ it as she is in need of __(II)______. Moreover, she is not in ___(III)_____ of the house. Jeanne and Gaston, a couple visit her with the aim of ___(IV)___ the Villa. While Jeanne is ___(V)____ about buying, Gaston detests the idea as he does not want his ___(VI)____ in that house. Also, he finds the asking price of _____(VII)__ to be expensive. When Jeanne and Juliette go around the house, another customer ____(VIII)____ and starts talking to Gaston ___(IX)___ him to be Juliette's husband. Gaston ___(X)____ a deal with the customer by which he is able to give ___(XI)___ to the owner and ____(XII)____ one thousand francs for himself.

Answer

(I) Sell	(II) money	(III) favour
(IV) buying	(V) enthusiastic	(VI) in-laws
(VII) 250 thousand francs	(VIII) walks in	(IX) taking
(X) strikes	(XI) 200 thousands francs	(XII) keep

Question 4. Answer the following questions briefly.

(a) Why does Jeanne want to buy a Villa?

Answer Jeanne wants to buy a Villa because she doesnot have a proper and commodious house. As per Gaston, she wants to buy a Villa for her parents and her sister's children to live in it.

(b) Why is Gaston not interested in buying the Villa in the beginning?

Answer Gaston is not interested in buying the Villa in the beginning because he does not want to settle Jeanne's parents and her sister's children in it. He is not fond of his in-laws and therefore he does not want to spend money for them.

(c) Mrs Al Smith makes many statements about the French. Pick out any two and explain them.

Answer "You, French people have a cute way of doing business ......"

(i) Mrs Al Smith means that French people are very clever at doing the business. They hide information in the beginning and reveal it in the end.

(ii) "Frenchmen usually have to consult about ten people before they get a more on ...."

Mrs Al Smith commented that French people cannot take their own decisions and therefore depend upon other people for decisions.

(d) Juliette says "....... now I have only one thought that is to get the wretched place off my hands. I would sacrifice it at any price." Does she stick to her words? Why/Why not?

Answer Juliette surely wanted to sell off her house as early as possible. As far as price is concerned, things worked in her favour. Mrs Al Smith bought the house in hurry from Gaston thinking him as the owner of the house. Gaston sold her the house in three hundred thousand francs and bought it from Juliette in two hundred thousand francs. Juliette therefore got the desired price for her Villa.

(e) Who is better in business - Juliette or Gaston ? Why?

Answer Gaston is better in business. He earned a clean profit of one hundred thousand francs without making any investment. On the other hand. Juliette was unable to convince Gaston to buy the Villa.

(f) Do you like/dislike Gaston? Give your reasons.

Answer Gaston is a good business man and a great opportunist. However, as a human being Gaston is not seem to be a person with good moral character. He is uncooperative and uncaring for his wife and her family. He talks rudely. He even cheats Mrs Al Smith and Juliette to earn the profit of one hundred thousand francs. He is a specimen of meanness, greediness, cleverness, craftiness and dishonesty.

Question 5. Read the following extracts and answer the question that follow by choosing the correct options.

(A) 'But the sign has been hanging on the gate for over a month now and I am beginning to be afraid that the day I bought it was when I was the real fool'.

(a) Why is Juliette disappointed?

(i) She is unable to get a role of cook in the films

(ii) Her maid is leaving as she has got a role in the films

(iii) She is unable to find a suitable buyer for her Villa

(iv) Gaston is offering a very low price for the Villa

Answer (iii)

(b) Why does she call herself a fool?

(i) She has decided to sell her Villa

(ii) There are no buyers for the Villa

(iii) She had bought the Villa for more than it was worth

(iv) The Villa was too close to the film studios

Answer (ii)

(B) 'But your parents would take possession of it, every year from the beginning of spring until the end of September. What's more they would bring the whole tribe of your sister's children with them'.

(a) What does Gaston mean by 'take possession'?

(i) Her parents would stay with them for a long time

(ii) Juliette's sister has many children

(iii) Gaston does not like children

(iv) Juliette's sister's children are badly behaved

Answer (i)

(C) 'While you were upstairs, I have been thinking a lot about your Papa and Mamma'.

(a) What is the discrepancy between what Gaston said earlier and what he says now?

(i) Earlier he did not want Juliette's parents to stay with them but now he is showing concern for them

(ii) Earlier he wanted Juliette's parents to stay with them but now he does not want them to come over

(iii) Earlier he wanted to buy a house for them but how he wants them to come and stay in their Villa

(iv) Earlier he stayed in Juliette's parents' Villa but now he wants them to stay with him and Juliette

Answer (i)

(b) What does the above statement reveal about Gaston's character?
   (i) He is selfish
   (ii) He is a opportunist
   (iii) He is a caring person
   (iv) He is hypocrite

   Answer (ii)

Question 6. Select words from the box to describe the characters in the play as revealed by the following lines. You may take the words from the box given on the next page.

	Lines from the Play	Speaker	Quality Revealed
(a)	One hundred thousand francs if necessary and that's only twice what it cost me.		greedy
(b)	If you don't want the house, tell me so at once and we'll say no more about it.		
(c)	No! I am very fond of your family, but not quite so fond as that.	Gaston	
(d)	Quite so, I have, but you haven't.		
(e)	I have never cared such a damned little about anybody's opinion.		
(f)	On the principle of people who like children and haven't any can always go and live near a school.		
(g)	The garden is not very large, but you see, it is surrounded by other gardens.	Juliette	
(h)	I will be philanthropic and let you have it for two hundred thousand.		
(i)	I have been thinking a lot about your Papa and Mamma. You see, I am really unselfish.		clever

cunning, clever, witty, smart, innocent, humorous, naughty overbearing, critical, domineering, disapproving, materialistic, dishonest, practical, greedy, cruel, boastful

Answer

	Lines from the Play	Speaker	Quality Revealed
(a)	One hundred thousand francs if necessary and that's only twice what it cost me.	Juliette	greedy
(b)	If you don't want the house, tell me so at once and we'll say no more about it.	Jeanne	innocent
(c)	No! I am very fond of your family, but not quite so fond as that.	Gaston	cunning, clever, smart
(d)	Quite so, I have, but you haven't.	Gaston	Boastful, cruel, domineering, naughty
(e)	I have never cared such a damned little about anybody's opinion.	Gaston	practical, cruel
(f)	On the principle of people who like children and haven't any can always go and live near a school.	Gaston	critical, witty, boastful
(g)	The garden is not very large, but you see, it is surrounded by other gardens.	Juliette	clever, humorous
(h)	I will be philanthropic and let you have it for two hundred thousand.	Juliette	materialistic
(i)	I have been thinking a lot about your Papa and Mamma. You see, I am really unselfish.	Gaston	clever, dishonest

Listening Task

Question 7. You are Jeanne, after coming home, you realise that the Villa was not actually bought and your husband has fooled both you and the landlady of the Villa. You are filled with rage, disgust and helplessness because of your husband's betrayal. Write your feelings in the form of a diary entry.

Answer

8:00 pm

Wednesday, 20th August, 2011

I felt befooled and cheated by my husband today. He not only cheated me but also the innocent landlady Juliette. She was selling her Villa at a modest amount. My husband craftily sold the Villa to Mrs Al Smith as its owner before buying it. He later on bought it and earned a clean profit of a hundred thousand francs. This way, he deceived Mrs Juliette. His greedy, cruel and mean behaviour really hurt me. He has made good profit in his business with the dowry given by my parents and now he has started befooling people to earn money. He has been cruel and mean to everyone around him, even to me, his wife. I definitely will do something to teach a lesson and deal with such a crooked person.

Term II

3

Fiction

The Man Who Knew Too Much

Alexander Baron

Synopsis

"The Man Who Knew Too Much" written by 'Alexander Baron' deals with story of an army person of an army training camp. Private Quelch is the nickname of the trainee who had great knowledge about the army things but could not won the admiration of his superior officers. His fellow trainees called him 'Professor' because of his knowledge. He was lanky and had stooping body. He used to always frowned through horn-rimmed spectacles.

Detailed Summary

Private Quelch

The narrator is also one of the trainees at the training camp. During the first lesson about the mechanism of a service rifle, professor corrected the sergeant. After the sergeant finished his lecture, he asked a number of questions to the professor. He answered them correctly and this enhanced his glory. He knew all the technical definitions, the parts of the rifle, its uses and cares. The sergeant asked him if he had any previous training. Professor replied that it was only intelligent reading.

Professor's Hard Work and Show Off

Professor used to work hard to achieve his goal. He borrowed training manuals to read them even late at nights. He drilled with great enthusiasm and energy. He was miraculously tireless. However, his show off was not loved by anyone. He walked like a guardsman in a canteen if an officer is insight. He lectured his companions about various aspects of human knowledge. At first, narrator and his friends admired him but soon they started avoiding him due to his show off. He would announce the mistakes of his fellow trainee in public to correct him.

Extraordinary Knowledge of Professor

The professor had great knowledge of an army aircrafts and military weapons. Once he identified an aircraft, only by his voice without even looking at it. All other trainees were trying to see it within the glare of Sun, whereas professor identified it by its sound only.

Turning Point in the Professor's Life

One day, during the lecture of Corporal Turnbull, professor poked in and interrupted as usual. Corporal Turnbull asked him to deliver the lecture. Professor delivered an unexceptionable lecture on grenade. After the lecture, Corporal Turnbull appointed him for the permanent cook house duties. This reward turned to be a joke and joy for all other trainees there.

Professor at Kitchen

One day narrator and his friend heard a familiar voice from the kitchen. It was the voice of professor. He was lecturing the other three cooks on unscientific and unhygienic method of peeling potatoes and wasting the vitamin values. The professor could never mend his nature of showing his superiority and knowledge. The narrator and his friend fled on this from the spot.

About the Author

Alexander Baron was born on 4th December, 1917 and died on 6th December, 1999. He was a British author and screenwriter. His notable works are 'From the City from the Plough' (1948), 'The Human Kind' (1953), 'The Low Life, (1963), 'King Dido' (1969), 'Queen of the East' (1956), 'Seeing Life' (1958), etc. Baron also served during Second World War in the Pioneer Corps of the British Army. After the war, he started his career as the Assistant Editor of 'The Tribune'.

Exercises

Question 1. The 'Professor' knew too much. How did he prove himself? Fill up the space with suitable examples from the story using the given clues.

(a) About muzzle velocity

Answer He told the sergeant, the exact muzzle velocity or speed at which bullet leaves the rifle as two thousand, four hundred and forty feet per second.

(b) After a thirty mile walk

Answer He looked miraculously tireless even after thirty miles walk. He drilled with enthusiasm and full energy. He always tried to impress his officers.

(c) His salute on payday

Answer When he saw officers, he would salute them by swinging his skinny arms and walking towards the canteen like a guardsman.

(d) The loud sound of a high flying invisible aeroplane

Answer He could judge the aircraft only by its sound. He identified a North American Harvard Trainer by its sound only, when the plane was invisible in the glare of Sun.

(e) About hand grenades

Answer One summer afternoon, Corporal Turnbull was giving lecture on hand grenades. He told the squad that a grenade's outside was divided up into a large number of fragments. These were to assist segmentation. Private Quelch at once spoke that these fragments were forty four in number. This irritated Corporal. But he controlled his irritation and asked professor to deliver the lecture. Then Professor delivered an unexceptional lecture on hand grenades.

(f) During cook house duties

Answer He did not stop his 'intelligent reading' for cookhouse duties. There also he lectured the other three cooks about the scientific and hygenic way of peeling potatoes without any waste of vitamin values.

Question 2. Based on your reading of the story, answer the following questions by choosing the correct options.

(a) Private Quelch was nick-named 'Professor' because of

(i) his appearance (ii) his knowledge
(iii) his habit of reading (iv) his habit of sermonising

Answer (ii)

(b) One could hammer nails into Corporal Turnbull without his noticing it because

(i) he was a strong and sturdy man
(ii) he was oblivious to his surroundings
(iii) he was a brave corporal
(iv) he was used to it

Answer (i)

(c) The author and his friend Trower fled from the scene as

(i) they had to catch a train
(ii) they could not stand Private Quelch exhibiting his knowledge
(iii) they felt they would have to lend a helping hand
(iv) they did not want to meet the cooks

Answer (ii)

Question 3. Answer the following questions briefly.

(a) What is a 'nickname'? Can you suggest another one for Private Quelch?

Answer Nickname is the second name or the informal name given to a person depending upon his most prominent character traits. The nickname is generally given by friends and colleagues. It reveals the humorous side of one's character. Private Quelch is nicknamed as 'Professor'. The other nicknames for him can be 'Mr Skinny', 'Mr Intelligent', 'Mr Nosy Poker' etc.

(b) Private Quelch looked like a 'Professor' when the author first met him at the training depot. Why?

Answer Private Quelch looked like a professor, because of his lean, lanky and stooping appearance. He wore horn-rimmed spectacles which added to his image of professor or a man of knowledge.

(c) What does the dark, sun-dried appearance of the Sergeant suggest about him?

Answer The Sergeant, by his appearance looked a man with great confidence and knowledge of the military. His sun-dried skin expressed that his knowledge is acquired through his practical and personal experience in the field.

(d) How was Private Quelch's knowledge exposed even further as the Sergeant's class went on?

Answer First of all professor told the exact muzzle velocity of the rifle to the sergeant. Later on sergeant put a series of questions to him, perhaps as revenge, which were all answered by professor correctly. Professor answered the questions with perfect technical definitions, detials about the parts of rifles, its uses and the ways to care for a rifle. He told the sergeant that he knew all this because of his intelligent reading.

(e) What did the Professor mean by intelligent reading?

Answer 'Intelligent reading' means reading the useful material with one has to memorise the knowledge. Moreover, attention, so that it can be applied in the life for enhancement of knowledge.

(f) What were the Professor's ambitions in the army?

Answer The Professor wanted to get a commission in the army. Before that he wanted to get a stripe *i.e.*, ribbons of rank in the force.

(g) Did Private Quelch's day-to-day practices take him closer towards his goal? How can you make out?

Answer No, Private Quelch's day to day practices were becoming more of a show off than an honest practice. In the beginning, all his fellow trainees used to respect him but later on they started avoiding him. Due to show off, he would insult his seniors as well as fellow colleagues unknowingly. No doubt, he had incomparable knowledge of defence forces but his way of achieving goal was not honest.

(h) Describe Corporal Turnbull.

Answer Corporal Turnbull was a young man. He was a sincere and serious person and not the man to be trifled with. He was the hero for all the trainees. All the trainees would talk that he is the toughest and the strongest man in the army and one can hammer nails in his body without his notice. He seems to be the man of self control, wisdom and understanding who did not lose his temper even by the interruptions of the professor during his class.

(i) How did Private Quelch managed to anger Corporal?

Answer During the Corporal's lecture, firstly Private Quelch interrupted him by telling the correct number of fragments on the granade. Later on, when Corporal resumed his lecture, Private Quelch interrupted again and asked him to start off with the characteristics of grenades. Corporal got angry on this and asked him to deliver the lecture.

(j) Do you think Private Quelch learnt a lesson when he was chosen for cook house duties? Give reasons for your answer.

Answer No, Private Quelch did not learn any lesson when he was chosen for cook house duties. He remained the same. In the kitchen, he started lecturing and advicing the cooks about their unscientific and unhygenic way of peeling potatoes which resulted in loss of vitamins.

Question 4. At first, Private Quelch was a hero in the eyes of his fellow soldiers. Support this observation with the help of suitable examples from the story.

Answer Yes, at first, Private Quelch was a hero in the eyes of his fellow soldiers. It was due to his knowledge, intelligence and hardwork. However, later on, when everybody realised that his knowledge, hardwork and intelligence are converting to show off, everybody began avoiding him.

He stayed up late at nights to read army manuals and magazines which had made his knowledge incomparable. He corrected the sergeant by telling the exact muzzle velocity and later on answered all the questions of asked by sergeant correctly. This raised his level in the eyes of the fellow soldiers.

He drilled with enthusiasm and he was miraculously tireless even at the end of thirty miles. He could identify the aircraft by its engine noise even without looking at it. He had the ambition to get commission, and everybody felt that he deserved it due to his knowledge, dedication and physical fitness. His fellow colleagues found his brainy and intelligent.

Question 5. Private Quelch knew 'too much'. Give reasons to prove that he was unable to win the admiration of his superior officers and colleagues in about 100 words.

Answer Private Quelch had the great knowledge about the army and even small thing srelated to it . But he failed to win admiration from his superior officers or colleagues. He was disliked among all due to his bad habit of over interference.

He would publicly correct the mistakes of colleague in order to show his own superiority. He spoke but not at the right time and to the right people. His act of correcting sergeant about the muzzle velocity and interrupting Corporal Turnbull for the correct way of giving lecture led to indiscipline in army.

Although, he was physically fit, had great knowledge and deserved commission, he ruined everything through his indiscipline and insensitive behaviour. His immature attitude deprived him from the admiration he could get from everyone around.

Question 6. (a) Write down the positive and the negative traits of the Private Quelch's character instances of the story.

Answer

Positive Traits	Instances from the Story
(i) Knowledge	Correcting muzzle velocity, identifying aircraft with its engines note, lecture on grenade.
(ii) Stamina	He was miraculously tireless even after the drill of thirty miles.
(iii) Hardwork	Reading army manuals and magazines even till late nights.
(iv) Perfection	Perfect knowledge of even small things, correcting even the way of peeling potatoes.
Negative Traits	**Instances from the Story**
(i) Immature talkativeness	Lecturing colleagues all the time, correcting even the trainers.
(ii) Over indulgence	Lecturing colleagues even when not required, speaking 'Thank You' even when the narrator was praised for cleaning his own hut.
(iii) Insensitive	Did not realise his mistakes even when Corporal Turnbull gave him permanent duties in cookhouse cook as a punishment.
(iv) Indiscipline	Interrupting the Sergeant and Corporal Turnbull to show off his knowledge during their lectures. He never bothered how his attitude and behaviour affected others.

(b) Now share your notes with the class. Add details if you need to.

Answer Students should exchange their notes and attempt this questions on their own.

(c) Attempt a character sketch of Private Quelch using your notes in about 100 words.

Answer Private Quelch was a trainee at an army training depot. He had lanky and stooping body. He wore horn-rimmed spectacles. He was nicknamed by his fellow trainees as 'Professor'. Everybody called him professor due to his peculiar personality and behaviour. He would work hard with perfection and had great knowledge and stamina. He could tirelessly drill for thirty miles and sing songs afterwards. He would even correct his trainers and senior officers during their lectures.

He was all the way deserving to get commission but he could not get admiration due to his insensitive and immature nature. He did not speak at the right time and to the right person. He interrupted his officers and corrected them during their lectures which made him disliked by all. His over indulgence and show off made him unpopular among his colleagues and undesirable man at the depot.

Writing Task

Question 7. You are the 'Professor'. Write a diary entry after your first day at the cookhouse, describing the events that led to this assignment, also express your thoughts and feelings about the events of the day in about 175 words.

Answer

4th November, 2012 10.30 pm

Sunday,

Today, I went to the cookhouse as I was appointed for the permanent cookhouse duties. First of all, I was confused and doubt the decision of Corporal Turnbull for assigning me these duties. But today, I got to know the reason.

The cooks at the cookhouse had no knowledge of cooking the food properly and preserving the nutritional values of the food. I had to taught them everything from peeling of potatoes to serve the food and later on washing the dishes. They were amazed on my knowledge and my practical approach. The Sergeant and Corporal Turnbull, both have realised my intelligence.

When I corrected the Sergeant, he asked me various other questions and tested my knowledge. Corporal Turnbull also realised my value during the lecture on hand grenade. Therefore, he decided to put me for the cookhouse duties, so that I could correct everything there.

As a result of his intelligent decision, today the food which was cooked under my directions was amazing. Everybody prepared it with joy.

I should thank Corporal Turnbull for giving this honour to me. However, when I was nominated to cookhouse duties, my fellow soldiers kept it as the joke for days, but I did not mind this.

I am confident that I shall prove my worth with great dedication and devotion to all my duties here. No doubt, in the coming time, I will change the whole outlook and the working culture of the cookhouse. With my expertise, everybody wiil be benefitted.

4

Keeping It From Harold

PG Wodehouse

Synopsis

PG Wodehouse had written the story 'Keeping It From Harold' based on Bramble's family. Harold was the son of a professional boxer, Bill Bramble. Harold was good, honest and kind by nature. He was a child prodigy. Therfore, Bill and his wife hid the truth of his father's profession from him. Somehow, Harold came to know about his father's profession and he behaved in an entirely different manner than expectations. Ironically what parents were hiding from their child turned out to be the greatest thing for Harold.

Detailed Summary

Harold, a Wonderful Child

Harold was busy in his studies when his mother asked him to go out for a walk by the river so that he would feel fresh. Harold was a boy blessed with utmost softness and intelligence. He was not like an ordinary child, he was different. He was a prodigy and a very well-behaved child. He had already won two prices at the Sunday school. He was completely devoted to his books and had an extraordinary pretty behaviour. This guy was completely admirable at school and locality.

Bill Bramble as a Father and His Nature

Mr Bramble was an excellent father who cared for his son a lot. On the advice of a senior curate of the parish and Major Percy Stokes (Mrs Bramble's brother) he kept the truth of his profession(being a boxer) away from his son. He never wanted him to feel disgraceful because of it.

Mr Bramble was a boxer by profession. However, in personal life he was very persuasive. He had always fallen in with suggestions without demur. By nature he was the mildest and the most obliged men. Even while keeping the name of his son Harold, he had withdrawn his suggestions with the utmost good humour in front of his wife's suggestions. He had thought the names before birth as John for boy, after Mr John L Sullivan, the famous boxer and Marie for girl, after Miss Marie Lloyd, the famous music hall artist. He was a likeable and excellent man.

Bill Bramble as a Professional

Before the birth of Harold, Bramble was a proud boxer. In his field, he was having advanced techniques which were praised in the London newspapers. He had the ability to pin his opponents. He was filled with satisfaction and felt elated when he found no man in London equal to him. Mr Bramble was popularly known as 'Young Porky' in London.

Trouble of Mr Bramble and Intelligence of Harold

When Harold came to his life, Mr Bramble became a furtive practiser of shady deeds. Earlier, he was delighted to see his name in any newspaper and now he feared at the sight of his name in print and hid it from Harold. He thought that Harold was not an ordinary boy and it mattered him a lot.

He was intelligent and sensitive. Both Bill and his wife believed Harold to be a boy of the superior order. Harold had supposed to beat the law of heredity. He had ran to intellect as his father had ran to muscle. He learnt to read and write amazingly quick and sang melodiously. Bill never wanted to tell his child about his profession as he did not want him to feel digraceful.

At the age of ten, Harold had already won the prize on spelling and dictation at the sunday school. He had grown in stature and intelligence. He was self centered child. Therefore, Mrs and Mr Bramble thought that it would not be a good idea to tell the boy that his father, whom he believed to be a commercial traveller was famous in London as a boxer by the name of 'Young Porky'.

Bramble's Professional Fight

Mrs Bramble was satisfied and relaxed in her mind about Harold's future. All the worries would end up next week when Bill would fight his last contest with American Murphy at the National Sporting Club. He was training himself for that contest at the White Hart. After the contest, he would start the work of an instructor in a school or a college.

He had respectability and sobriety which were regarded essential for that job. That job was honourful and soft. While in a relaxed mood Mrs Bramble was darning the socks, Major Percy and Mr Bramble entered the house. She asked Mr Bramble surprisingly that what he was doing there.

He should had been at the White Hart training, Mr Bramble told her that he was not going to fight. Mrs Bramble asked what would he had done to the money, he borrowed from her. Mrs Bramble said that she never liked her profession but it gave a good money.

This money had enabled them to provide the best education to Harold. During this fight also, he would get £ 500 if won and £ 120 if lost. This money was to be a blessing that would give Harold a better start in life. She worried what would happen if he didnot fight. She began to sob.

Bramble Gave Reason of not Fighting

Mr Bramble told his wife that he was thinking of Harold while returning from White Hart. The news of the fight would publish in newspapers with photos. If Harold would watch them, it would be trouble for them. Mr Fisher came to their house, he was angry that Mr Bramble had quit the contest.

He accused as for that and asked Mr Bramble to go with him. Mr Bramble gave him the reason for quitting the fight and refused to fight on Monday. He told Mr Fisher that Harold would die of shame and disgrace if he came to know about his father's profession. As, they were keeping this fact from Harold. Mr Fisher had tears in his eyes after hearing this.

Harold Came Back and Mr Fisher's Reaction

While these four elders were talking, Harold came back and heard his name. He asked his father what he thought about his thinking. He also asked them whether they had hear his piece of poetry or not. Everybody was stunned and shocked and became quiet. Three of the four adults faces showed consternation while the eyes of Mr Fisher showed nasty and steely expression.

He wanted to tell Harold everything. The other three tried to stop him but he ignored them. He told everything to Harold and Bill sank into a chair. Percy tried to explain Harold that he should not think worse about his father for being a man of wrath. Neither he should feel ashamed. Bill started to explain Harold that he had already left the profession.

Harold's Reaction

Which he had Harold drew a deep breath. He wondered what would happen to his two bob. Which he had betted with Dicky Saunders. It was that Jimmy Murphy would not last even for ten rounds. He told his father that he would now lose the bet and it was a rotten thing they kept that from him. He told that a fellow in school had been displaying Phill Scott's autograph.

Other students looked at him awfully. They called Harold 'Goggles'. Harold said that now nobody would be able to call him 'Googles' if they knew about his father. He even added that his father should fight to Sampson for the Lonsdale belt and also Ted Richards. He also asked for a picture of his father at boxing so that he could show it to his friends.

Bill's Decision

On hearing all this Mr Fisher asked Mr Bramble to get back to White Hart for training and give up the idea of quitting. Bramble followed him quiety. Both Mrs Bramble and Harold were cheerful at the moment. They exchanged sweet words thereafter.

About the Author

Sir Pelham Grenville Wodehouse, KBE was born on October 15, 1881 and died on February 14, 1975. He was a comic writer. He was enormously successful and acknowledged as the master of English prose. He has been known even today for his the Jeeves and Blandings Castle novels and short stories. Moreover, he wrote 15 plays and of about 250 lyrics for some 30 musical comedies. He wrote the lyrics for the hit song "Bill" in Kern's Show Boat (1927) and many other songs.

Exercises

Question 1. Before you read 'Keeping It From Harold', the teacher will encourage you to answer or discuss the following.

(a) What are the different weight categories in Boxing?

Answer The different weight categories in Boxing are the following

(i)	Light Fly	46 to 48 kg
(ii)	Fly	48 to 51 kg
(iii)	Bantam	51 to 54 kg
(iv)	Feather	54 to 57 kg
(v)	Light	57 to 60 kg
(vi)	Light Welter	60 to 63.5 kg
(vii)	Welter	64 to 71 kg
(viii)	Middle	71 to 75 kg
(ix)	Light Heavy	75 to 81 kg
(x)	Heavy	81 to 91 kg
(xi)	Super Heavy	above 91 kg

(b) Have you ever heard the song whose lyrics go like...."He floats like a butterfly and stings like a bee"? Who does 'he' refer to? He is also known as 'The Greatest' boxer of all time. What was his original name? How many times did he win the World Heavyweight Belt?

Answer Yes, I have heard this song. It is about the World's Heavyweight Boxing Champion Muhammad Ali. His original name is Cassius Clay. He won the World Heavyweight Belt three times.

(c) Find out from your friend if he/she watches WWE and who is his/her favourite wrestler. Also find out why he/she likes this wrestler.

Answer I discussed about WWE with my friend. His favourite wrestler is 'The Great Khali'.

He likes Khali because he is the first Indian who has made our country proud by making a significant position in World Wrestling Entertainment (WWE). His original name is Dalip Singh Rana. He is not only a professional wrestler but also an actor and a power lifter.

(d) Discuss with your friend as to why these wrestlers have such a large fan following. Has the perception of people changed over the century with respect to those who fight in the ring?

Answer These wrestlers have a large fan following them. The reasons behind this are

(i) Sheer entertainment is involved in these games.
(ii) Adventure and suspense is involved in these games.
(iii) Amazement regarding the bodies of these players.
(iv) How the players maintain their body and keep themselves fit and agile.
(v) Immense excitement regarding the winner.

The perception of people have changed over the last century with respect to these fighters in the ring. It is more due to the fact that these champion boxers have become star celebrities. Now-a-days Boxing, Wrestling, Kabaddi, etc have attracted more and more people. In our country, the popularity came after the great achievement of Vijendra Singh and Sushil Kumar in Beijing Olympics. Now, Boxing and Wrestling as games have reached the villages as well. Millions of aspirants are now attracted to them not only in India but also all over the world.

Question 2. Based on your reading of the story, answer the following questions by choosing the correct option.

(a) Mrs Bramble was a proud woman because
  (i) she was the wife of a famous boxer
  (ii) she had motivated her husband
  (iii) she was a good housewife
  (iv) she was the mother of a child prodigy

Answer (iv)

(b) "The very naming of Harold had caused a sacrifice on his part". The writer's tone here is
  (i) admiring
  (ii) assertive
  (iii) satirical
  (iv) gentle

Answer (iii)

(c) Harold had defined the laws of heredity by
  (i) becoming a sportsperson
  (ii) being good at academics
  (iii) being well-built and muscular
  (iv) respecting his parents

Answer (ii)

(d) Harold felt that he was deprived of the respect that his classmates would give him as

(i) they did not know his father was the famous boxer, 'Young Porky'
(ii) his hero, Jimmy Murphy had not won the wrestling match
(iii) he had not got Phil Scott's autograph
(iv) Sid Simpson had lost the Lonsdale belt

Answer (i)

Question 3. Answer the following questions

(a) What was strange about the manner in which Mrs Bramble addressed her son? What did he feel about it?

Answer Mrs Bramble referred to herself in third person while talking to Harold. Harold felt little angry on this. He would consider it as if his mother thought of him as a child.

(b) Why was it necessary to keep Harold's father's profession a secret from him?

Answer Harold was a gifted child. Unlike his boxer father, he was very intelligent and soft-spoken child. Mrs and Mr Bramble did not want him to feel disgrace after knowing his father's profession. Therefore, they hid it from him.

(c) When Mr Bramble came to know that he was to become a father what were some of the names he decided upon? Why?

Answer Mr Bramble wanted to name his child on the names of some famous personalities. He thought that if he had a boy, he would name him as John, after John L Sullivan, the American boxing legend. If they had a girl, he would name her as Marie, after Miss Marie Lloyd, the famous music hall artist.

(d) Describe Mr Bramble as he has been described in the story.

Answer Mr Bramble has been described as a mild and obliged man. He was persuasive, a thorough gentleman and a loving father. He had sacrificing nature although his profession was wrathful. He was a likeable person with excellent behaviour.

(e) Why was Mrs Bramble upset when she came to hear that Bill had decided not to fight?

Answer Mrs Bramble was upset because that would mean that he would earn no money. She believed that they need money to give a good start to Harold's life. She also reminded Mr Bramble that he had to return her the money he had borrowed from her.

(f) Who was Jerry Fisher? What did he say to try and convince Bill to change his mind?

Answer Jerry Fisher was Bill's trainer at White Hart. He tried in all ways to convince Bill to fight. When he saw that Bill was not ready to fight because of his son, he told the truth to his son, Harold. He told Harold that his father was a professional boxer.

(g) How did Harold come to know that his father was a boxer?

Answer Harold came to know this truth from Jerry Fisher. He told Harold that his father was a famous boxer and known to everybody as 'Young Porky'.

(h) Why was Harold upset that his father had not told him about his true identity? Give reasons.

Answer Harold was upset that his father had not told him about his true identity because he was bullied by his friends by the name 'Googles'. He said if it would had known to him earlier, no body could ridiculed him. Secondly, he had betted his friends on boxing event. He thought he would lose the bet if his father would not fight.

(i) Do you agree with Harold's parents' decision of hiding from him the fact that his father was a boxer? Why/Why not?

Answer I agree with Harold's parents decision of hiding from him the real nature of his father's profession. Mr Bramble was a father who did not want to hurt his son's feelings. But on the other hand, I feel that there was some miscommunication between the parents and the son. They never tried to know whether he would like it or not. They made a misconception. This would have been avoided. They would have talked to their son and understand him better.

Question 4. The sequence of events has been jumbled up. Rearrange them and complete the given flow chart.

1. Major Percy and Bill come to the house.
2. Harold comes to know that his father is a boxer.
3. Bill tells his wife that he is doing it for Harold.
4. Jerry Fisher tries to convince Bill to reconsider.
5. Mrs. Bramble is amazed to think that she has brought such a prodigy as Harold into the world.
6. Harold wants to know what will happen to the money he had bet on Murphy losing.
7. Mrs. Bramble is informed that Bill had decided not to fight.

8. Mrs. Bramble resumes work of darning the sock.
9. Harold is alone with his mother in their home.

Answer The correct sequence of sentence is 9, 5, 8, 1, 7, 3, 4, 2, 6.

Question 5. Choose extracts from the story that illustrates the characters of these people in it.

Person	Extracts from the story	What this tell us about their characters
Mrs Bramble	(Para 12) "Bill we must keep it from Harold"	She was not honest and open with her son, concerned mother.
Mr Bramble	(Para 33)	
Percy	(Para 109)	
Jerry Fisher		

Answer

Person	Extracts from the story	What this tell us about their character
Mrs Bramble	(Para 12) "Bill we must keep it from Harold"	She was not honest and open to her son, concerned mother.
Mr Bramble	(Para-33) The scales have fallen down from his eyes.	Honest and simple minded man.
Percy	(Para 109) There was a crooning winningness in Percy's voice.	Man who was sure of winning upto the last time.
Jerry Fisher		Straight forward, confident and less sensitive too.

Listening Task

Question 6. The teacher will ask the students to answer these questions based on an interview given by the legendary WWE wrestler, Kane to Chris Carle of IGN. The students are to listen to the interview.

1. What were the video games that Kane liked playing earlier and which games later?

   Answer Kane was fond of Halo 2 and Ghost Racon earlier. Later he loved to play THQ's Raw *vs* Samachdown 2006.

2. Who was Kane's favourite wrestler when he was first getting into wrestling and who were some of the other wrestlers who influenced him into taking up wrestling?

   Answer Undertaker was his favourite wrestler and the wrestlers who influenced him were Randy Savage, Ricky Steamboat, Rio Flair, Four Horsemen and Hulk Hogan.

3. How according to Kane had the WWE changed in the past ten years?

   Answer According to Kane, the WWE had become a product of television. The format had also changed due to the competition from the formely WCW. Business also had grown manifold.

4. Does Kane prefer performing with the mask or without the mask?

   Answer Kane prefers performing without mask. He feels that he can do unlimited in his performance. With the mask he has to rely more on his body language.

5. Why does Kane wrestle these days even though he has accomplished almost everything?

   Answer For him, wrestling is simply a fun to Kane and he wants to entertain his fans.

6. What is your impression of Kane as a person after you have heard this interview?

   Answer Kane is a wrestler in the true sense and a man of principles. Secondly, he has a love and respect for his fans also.

Writing Task

Question 7. Many people are of the opinion that violent, physical sports such as boxing, kick boxing and wrestling, to name a few should be banned while others think otherwise. Express your opinion on the topic by either writing in favour of banning these sports or against banning them. While writing, you should also include the rebuttal to your questions. Try not to go beyond 200 words.

Answer

Physical Sports should not be Banned

Physical sports involve the use of muscle power. Often people say that these sports lead to violence. However, this is a myth that violence can be caused by any sport. If a sport is watched and played with a true sportsman spirit, it can not cause voilence.

Its the propaganda of voilence that should be banned. There is an urge to develop a proper attitude among people for watching these games. Whenever people get too much involved in a sport, violence may take place. e.g., during India and Pakistan cricket match, huge wrath is seen from the supporters of the loosing team.

Does it mean that cricket should also be banned? Sports are made for physical exercise and mental relaxation. Banning sports is not the solution. Violence is the result of increasing indiscipline, unhealthy competition, egoist attitudes among us. There is a high need to ban this negativity and develop positive personality traits. Development of humanism and peace of mind is required. Then only one can understand that sports are the medium of entertainment and relaxation for the spectators and the medium of physical fitness for the players.

5

Best Seller

O Henry

Synopsis

The 'Best Seller' is written by O Henry which tells the story about John A Pescud who is a travelling salesman. He criticises best seller novels and called them away from reality. Ironically, Pescud does the same thing which he criticises and opposes. He is reading the best seller 'The Rose Lady and Trevelyan', but he himself is 'Trevelyan'. Pescud as he relates the story of his life to the narrator, it is like the hero of the novel.

Detailed Summary

About the Best Seller

The narrator was going to Pittsburgh for business when he met John A Pescud, an old acquaintance in the chair car. He was reading the novel, one of the best sellers, "The Rose Lady and Trevelyan". The conversation between them started with the topics like rain, prosperity, health, residence and destination. Pescud is the travelling salesman of a plate-glass company.

He feels that in his home town a man should be law-abiding and decent. He was a small man with wide smile, and an eye that seemed to be fixed upon that little spot on the end of your nose. He believed that his plate glass is the most important commodity in the world. Pescud did not like the Best Seller novels like the one he was reading.

He told the story of the novel in which the hero is an American swell who felt in love with a royal princess from Europe who was travelling under an alias and followed her to her father's kingdom. The princess reminded him of the status gap between both of them.

Pescud and The Narrator's Views on Real Life and Fiction

Pescud said that these love stories were only fictional. In real life, a person generally marry the girl of his own status. The narrator said that he has understood what he wanted to say. He wanted fiction writers to be consistent with their scenes and characters. He did not want rich men mix with ordinary men, like high officials and farmers and English dukes with shell fish catching people. Now, the narrator asked Pescud about his life, job, family etc.

Pescud Tells About Himself and Meeting the Girl of Choice

Pescud told the narrator that his salary had raised twice since they had last met and he had got a commission too. He had bought some property. He would get some company's share too in the following year. He said that he had been on the line of 'General Prosperity'. Then the narrator asked him about his to-be-wife and Pescud began to tell his story.

He said that he was going to Cincinnati around 18 months ago. There he saw the most beautiful lady he had ever seen, reading a book. Pescud was watching and even kept aside the job for her. She changed cars at Cincinnati and took a sleeper to Lousiville. Then travelled through Shelbyville Frankford and Lexington. He found it hard to keep with her as trains moved in and out. However, he never lost track of her. She got off at Virginia in the evening.

There she met a tall old man, with a smooth face and white hair, looking as proud as Julius Caesar. They went in a gate on top of the hill to a huge house as big as the capitol at Washington. Pescud found a fine hotel in the village called 'The Bay View House'. From the hotel owner he came to know that the house belonged to Colonel Allyn, the biggest man in Virginia. That girl was his daughter who had been to Illinois to see her sick aunt.

Meeting between Pescud and the Girl

On the third day of his stay in the village Pescud managed to meet the girl. He told her about himself. She smiled at him and even blushed. She also told him that she had never talked to anyone like that before. She told Pescud that she had seen him almost on every train and he was going to speak to her.

The girl told Pescud that her family was living there for almost hundred years. Moreover, her father never allowed anyone to talk to her. If he came to know that she had talked to him, she would be locked in a room. The girl told her name as Jessie.

Pescud Meets Colonel Allyn, Girl's Father

Pescud went to the big house to meet Colonel Allyn, next morning. He found that the big house did not had much furniture. The Colonel asked Pescud to sit down. Pescud told Colonel how he followed his daughter and reached there. Pescud expected that he would be thrown out of the house but their conversation went for two a hours. Pescud asked Colonel to let him marry his daughter.He told everything about himself to Colonel.

He told that his family had always lived in and around Pittsburgh. One of his uncle was in real-estate business. He could inquire about them in smoky town. He referred to Sir Courtenay Pescud in the times of Charles. Colonel did not know about him. Colonel told him the story of fox-hunting.

Pescud Tells About His Marriage

After two evenings, Pescud got the chance to meet Colonel's daughter Miss Jessie. Pescud heard the porter's sound as Coketown came. He got ready to get down. He added that he married Colonel's daughter a year ago and build a house in East End. The colonel too was there and would be at gate to tell him another story.

Reason to Visit Coketown

The narrator told Pescud that he would not find enough business of plate-glass in Coketown because of its rough hill-side. Pescud said that he had not came there for business. It was to get some cuttings and blossoms of petunias for Jessie as she liked them while coming from Philadelphia and wanted to grow them at her house.

End Note of the Story

The train moved forward. The narrator saw the best seller lying down. He picked it up and set it down carefully on the floor of the car. He smiled and saw that life had no geographical bounds. His friend was going through a similar love story in real life as there was one in that best seller. He wished good luck to Pescud for getting flowers for her princess and at the same time wished good luck for Trevelyan. Pescud and Trevelyan were one and the same person, the hero of the best seller.

About the Author

O Henry is the other name of William Sydney Porter who was born in 1862 and died in 1910. He was an American writer who wrote short stories. He was best known for irony and surprising twists in his story. He was one of the most popular writers of America who wrote over 500 short stories in dozens of widely read periodicals. Many American movies and television programmes are made on his stories. In 1919, the O Henry Memorial Awards founded by society of Arts and Science which are given to the best American short story published each year.

Exercises

Question 1. Before you read the story write down the answer to these questions

(a) Which was the latest book that you read?

Answer I have read the book 'Gulliver's Travels' recently.

(b) Who was the author?

Answer Jonathan Swift

(c) Who were the main characters?

Answer Gulliver, the Emperor of Lilliput, Reldresal, Flimnap, the Farmer, the King, the Queen, Glumdalclitch William Prichard etc.

(d) When did you read the book?

Answer I read the book one month ago.

(e) How long did you take to complete reading it?

Answer It took a week to read the book.

(f) What genre did it belong to?

Answer This book is a work of fiction.

(g) Why would/wouldn't you recommend it?

Answer I would suggest everybody to read the book. It is the story of a brave person who loves voyages. He faces lots of problems during his journey but with his courage and luck he overcomes all the difficulties. It is an entertaining book.

Question 2. Based on your reading of the story, answer the following questions by choosing the correct option.

(a) The narrator says that John was "......... of the stuff that heroes are not often lucky enough to be made of." His tone is sarcastic because

(i) he hated John
(ii) he felt that John was a threat to him
(iii) John was not particularly good looking
(iv) nobody liked John

Answer (iii)

(b) Pescud felt that best-sellers were not realistic as

(i) American farmers had nothing in common with European princesses
(ii) men generally married girls from a similar background
(iii) American men married girls who studied in America
(iv) American men did not known fencing and were beaten by the Swiss guards

Answer (ii)

(c) **"Bully"**, said Pescud brightening at once. He means to say that

(i) he is a bully
(ii) his manager is a bully
(iii) he is being bullied by his co-workers
(iv) he is doing very well at his job

Answer (iv)

(d) The narrator says that life has no geographical bounds implying that

(i) human beings are essentially the same everywhere
(ii) boundaries exists only one maps
(iii) one should Work towards the good of mankind
(iv) he was happy to travel to other countries

Answer (i)

Question 3. Answer the following questions briefly.

(a) One day last summer the author was travelling to Pittsburg by his chair car, what does he say about his co-passenger?

Answer Author said that most of the passengers were ladies. Most of them were wearing brown-silk dresses cut with square rocks, laced ones and with dotted veils. There was a usual number of men. They were going anywhere on any business.

(b) Who was the passenger of chair No.9? What did he suddenly do?

Answer John A Pescud was on chair 9. He was an old acquaintance of the narrator the and a travelling salesman of a plate-glass company. He suddenly hurled a book on the floor between his chair and the window.

(c) What was John A Pescud's opinion about best sellers? Why?

Answer John's opinion was that all the best sellers were of the kind where the hero was a wealthy American man who loves a royal princess from Europe. The man also travelled under a false name to the girl's father's kingdom. He strongly felt that these novels are away from reality and purely fictional.

(d) What does John say about himself since his last meeting with the author?

Answer John told about himself that his salary had been raised twice and he had also got commission. He had bought himself some property also. He would also get his company's share next year. He had built a house at the East End and had married too.

(e) How did John's first meeting with Jessie's father go? What did the author tell him?

Answer John's meeting with Jessie's father for the first time was quite well. He honestly told how he followed his daughter and asked to marry her. He felt that Colonel will throw him out of the window. But soon they became comfortable and they kept on talking for two hours.

(f) Why did John get off to Coketown?

Answer John A Pescud got down at Coketown because he wanted cuttings and blossoms of petunia flowers for his wife. She wanted them because she liked them a lot and wanted to grow them in her garden.

(g) John is a hypocrite. Do you agree with this statement? Substantiate your answer.

Answer I think John is a hypocrite. He criticises the plot of the best sellers and called it unrealistic and fictional. However, he had demonstrated the same thing from his own life. The best seller, "The Rose Lady and the 'Trevelyan' has the same plot as the life of Pescud. In a way, he himself is 'Trevelyan'. He thinks that a man will always marry the girl of same class and status. But he himself married a rich girl.

(h) Describe John A Pescud with reference to the following points

1. Physical appearance
2. His philosophy on behaviour
3. His profession
4. His first impression of his wife
5. His success

Answer

1. **Physical Appearance**
   John Pescud was a small man with a wide smile. He had an eye which seemed to be fixed upon the little red spot on the end of the nose.

2. **His Philosophy on Behaviour**

   He felt that a man ought to be decent and law-abiding.

3. **His Profession**

   He was a travelling salesman. At present, he is a travelling salesman of a plate-glass company named Cambria Steel Works.

4. **His First Impression of his Wife**

   He found her to be the best, beautiful and the finest looking lady in the world he had ever seen. She was not very spectacular but had all the attributes of an ideal wife.

5. **His Success**

   Pescud had satisfactory success in his life. In two years he got two times rise in salary and also got a commission. He has bought a house for himself and would be buying company's share next year. He had married the girl whom he loved.

Question 4. Complete the flow chart in the correct sequence as it happens in the story.

Hint It begins from the time John Pescud first saw Jessie till the time they marry.

1. Jessie takes a sleeper to Louisville.
2. Pescud sees a girl (Jessie) reading a book in the train.
3. Pescud speaks to the girl (Jessie) for the first time.
4. Pescud follows her but finds it difficult to keep up.
5. Pescud goes to the village to find out about the mansion.
6. Jessie arrives at Virginia.
7. Pescud meets Jessie's father.
8. They get married a year later.
9. Pescud instantly gets attracted to the girl (Jessie).
10. Jessie informs Pescud that her father would not approve of them meeting.
11. They meet alone two days later.

Answer The correct sequence as it happened in the story, is

2, 9, 4, 1, 6, 5, 3, 10, 7, 11 and 8.

Question 5. Irony refers to the use of words to convey a meaning that is opposite of their literal meaning. Working in pairs, bring out the irony in the following

(a) The title of the story, "The Best Seller".

Answer "The Best Seller" should be realistic and the story of public. However, the story of Pescud is not the story as per the definition of "Best Seller".

(b) Pescud said, "When people in real life marry, they generally hunt up somebody in their own station. A fellow usually picks out a girl who went to the same high school and belonged to the same singing society that he did."

Answer Pescud said that people generally marry within their own kith and kin who belong to their own society. However, Pescud himself did not follow this in his own life. He married daughter of Colonel Allyn, a noble man while he himself is an ordinary salesman of a plate-glass company.

(c) The name Trevelyan.

Answer Trevelyan is the hero of the novel, 'The Rose lady and Trevelyan'. Pescud criticised Trevelyan in the beginning of the story but Pescud and Trevelyan were one and the same person.

Question 6. A newspaper reporter hears of the marriage of Pescud and Jessie. He interviews them and writes an article for the paper entitled: A Modern Romance.
Working in groups of four write the article.

Answer Meant as group activity. You can take the article given below as sample.

A Modern Romance

The dictionary meaning of the word 'romance' is "relationship between two people who are in love with each other". The romance of modern age is away from the hurdles of caste, colour, creed, status and traditions. There is no weightage given to these things by the young people. Pescud saw Jessie, liked her and decided to marry her without knowing anything about her. He forgot his job and work and followed her to home.

Once he met her outside the house, talked to her and decided to meet her father for marriage proposal. However, there is nothing wrong with that if two people love each other irrespective of their social status like Pescud and Jessie. Pescud cared for Jessie's need and happiness. He especially went to Coketown to bring cutting and blossoms of her favourite flower Petunia. If every body cares for his or her partner like this, romance will bind them forever.

Poetry

4

Lord Ullin's Daughter

Thomas Campbell

Synopsis

'Lord Ullin's daughter' is a ballad written by 'Thomas Campbell'. The poet revealed the story of two lovers, their elopement and their death. A Scottish chieftain and his beloved eloped from the wrathful father of the girl. They fled through the stormy river and met the tragic end. They were caught in the violent, englufing waves and meet their end. Girl's father was standing on the beach of the fatal river but before he could do anything the violent storm killed the girl and her lover. Father's wrath changed to grief when he saw his daughter dying. He wanted to get back his daughter and forgive her. He cried, but all went in vain.

Detalied Summary

Couple Flee from the House

A chieftain with his beloved reached the bank of the river in a stormy night. He asked the boatman to help them cross over the river. Both, the chieftain and his beloved were terribly afraid and wanted to run away as soon as possible. The chieftain was ready to give a silver pound to the boatman. At first the boatman was not ready to cross the sea as it was a stormy night and river lochgyle became terribly stormy. The lovers were running for three continuous days and the girl's father, Lord Ullin's men were after them to catch them. The boy was the chief of Ulva Isle and knew that he would be killed if found by Lord Ullin.

He explained the boatman that if he would be murdered, then nobody would be there to make his lovely bride happy. Then boatman agree to cross the river, not for the silver coin but for the sake of his beautiful wife.

Growing Storm

The storm had grown more terrible. The boatsman and the lovers start crossing the stormy river. The sky was becoming darker, and darker and the water waves were moving to and fro like an angry devil. The wind blew wildly. Lord Ullin's armed horsemen were coming to catch them through the valley.

The River Won the Fight

The girl was worried about her beloved and becoming impatient to move from there. She asked the boatman to hurry up and move fast. She would not like to face her angry father, instead she would prefer to meet the angry sky.

They started sailing in the river but the tempest was too strong for the human beings to face and storm gathered over them. They continued to sail and the storm drowned them. Lord Ullin's reached the shore and found himself unable to save his daughter.

Change of Lord Ullin's Mind

Lord Ullin's anger changed to grief and now he wanted to get back his daughter. He said that he would forgive her highland chief. He was lamenting on the shore and watched his daughter stretching one arm towards him for help and another round her beloved. He saw his own beloved daughter drowning before his own wrath changed into wailing.

About the Poet

Thomas Campbell was born in Scotland on July 27, 1777. He was chiefly remembered for his sentimental poetry dealing specially with human affairs. He was one of the initiations of a plan to found what became the university of London. In 1799, he wrote 'The Pleasures of Hope' a traditional 18th century survey in heroic couplets. He also produced several patriotic war songs "Ye Mariners of England", "The Soldier's Dream", "Hohen Linden" and in 1801, "The Battle of the Baltic" etc. He died in Boulogene on June 15, 1844.

Exercises

Question 1. On the basis of your understanding of the poem, answer the following questions by ticking the correct choice.

(a) Lord Ullin's daughter and her lover are trying to
   (i) escape the wrath of her father
   (ii) settle in a distant land
   (iii) challenge the storm in the lake
   (iv) trying to prove their love for each other

Answer (i)

(b) The boatman agrees to ferry them across because
   (i) he has fallen in love with Lord Ullin's daughter
   (ii) he wants to avenge Lord Ullin
   (iii) he has lost his love
   (iv) he is sorry for the childlike innocence of the lady

Answer (iv)

(c) The mood changes in the poem. It transforms from
   (i) happiness to fear
   (ii) anxiety to grief
   (iii) fear to happiness
   (iv) love to pain

Answer (ii)

(d) The shore of Lochgyle has been referred to as 'fatal shore'! The poetic device used here is
   (i) metaphor
   (ii) simile
   (iii) transferred epithet
   (iv) onomatopoeia

Answer (ii)

Question 2. In pairs, copy and complete the summary of the poem with suitable words/expressions.

A Scottish Chieftain and his beloved were ____(I)____ from her wrathful father. As they reached the shores, the ____(II)____ told a boatman to ____(III)____ them across Lochgyle. He asked him to do it quickly because if ____(IV)_____ found them, they would kill him. The boatman ____(V)_____ to take them not for the _____(VI)_____ that the Chieftain offered but for his ____(VII)_____. By this time, the storm had ____(VIII)____ and a wild wind had started blowing. The sound of ___(IX)____ could be heard close at hand. The lady urged the boatman ____(X)____ as she did not want to face an angry father.

Their boat left the ___(XI)___ and as it got caught in the stormy sea, Lord Ullin reached the deadly ____(XII)____. His anger changed to wailing when he saw his daughter ___(XIII)___. He asked her to return to the shore. But, it was ____(XIV)____ as the stormy sea claimed his daughter and her lover.

Answer (I) fleeing (II) chieftain (III) ferry (IV) Lord Ullin's men (V) agreed (VI) money (VII) beloved (VIII) grown loud (IX) trampest (X) to hurry up (XI) stormy land (XII) shore (XIII) was drowning (XIV) in vain

Question 3. Why does Lord Ullin's daughter defy her father and elope with her lover?

Answer Lord Ullin's daughter defied her father and eloped with her lover because her father was not ready for their marriage and wanted to kill her beloved, chief of Ulva.

Question 4. Give two characteristics of the boatman who ferries the couple across the sea?

Answer The boatman who ferried the couple across the sea was

(i) kind hearted and straight forward.

(ii) helpful and away from greed of money.

Question 5. "Imagery" refers to something that can be perceived through more than one of the senses. It uses figurative language to help from mental pictures. Campbell used vivid, diverse and powerful imagery to personify the menacing face of nature. Pick out expressions that convey the images of anger in the following stanzas.

Stanza 6 . ____________________

Stanza 7 . 'Water-wraith was shrieking'

. ____________________

Stanza 9 . ____________________

Stanza 10 . ____________________

. 'Stormy land'

Stanza 13 . ____________________

Stanza 14 . ____________________

Answer Stanza 6 : waves are raging white

Stanza 7 : 'Scrowl of heaven' 'Waterwraith was shrieking'

Stanza 9 : raging of the skies

Stanza 10 : stormy sea

Stanza 13 : stormy water

Stanza 14 : loud waves lash'd the shore

Question 6. Read the following lines and answer the questions that follow

"His horsemen hard behind us ride;
Should they our steps discover,
Then who will cheer my bonny bride
When they have slain her lover?"

(a) Who is 'his' in line 1? Who does 'us' refer to?
(b) Explain 'cheer my bonny bride'.
(c) Why would the lover be slain?

Answer

(a) 'His' refers to Lord Ullin and 'us' refers to Lord Ullin's daughter and her beloved.
(b) 'Bonny bride' means 'attractive woman'. Chieftain is worried that if he dies, then who will look after his beloved.
(c) He would be slain because he eloped with Lord Ullin's daughter. Lord Ullin was against their relation and did not give permission to his daughter to marry her lover. He wanted to punish the chieftain.

Question 7. "The water-wraith was shrieking". Is the symbolism in this line a premonition of what happens in the end? Give reasons for your answer. (Stanza 7)

Answer The anger of water or storm was increasing continuously. Yes, it is the premonition of the climax of the lover. That stormy river and the angry weather proved as fatal for the two lovers. Both of them drowned in the fury of the river.

Question 8. The poet uses words like 'adown' and 'rode' which contain harsh consonants. Why do you think the poet has done this? (Stanza 8)

Answer The poet uses words like 'adown' and 'rode' to emphasise the anger and fury of the enemies (armed men) chasing his daughter and chieftain.

Question 9. In stanza 10, the poet says

The boat has left a stormy land,
A stormy sea before her, ...

(a) In both lines, the word "stormy" assumes different connotations. What are they?
(b) The lady faces a dilemma here. What is it? What choice does she finally make?

Answer

(a) The land was 'stormy' because of the angry father whereas the sea was angry due to the weather. The girl had to either face the storm of father's rage or the river.

(b) The dilemma is that the lady has 'storm' on both her sides. She can not make a choice between her father and lover. She can not return as there is 'storm' at home. She can not go forward as there is terrible sea storm too. Finally she chosen to face the sea storm as she thinks it better to be killed with her lover than to live without him.

Question 10.

(a)"Lord Ullin reached that fatal shore" just as his daughter left it. (Stanza 11) Why is the shore called fatal?

(b) Why does Lord Ullin's wrath change into wailing on seeing his daughter?

Answer

(a) "Lord Ullin reached the fatal shore". The shore is called fatal because that shore became the ultimate fate of the two lovers. They lost their lives and the story of their love ended there.

(b) Lord Ullin's wrath changed into wailing due to love and affection for his daughter. His daughter was stretching her arm towards him for aid but he was unable to help or save his daughter.

Question 11. "One lovely hand she stretch'd for aid." Do you think Lord Ullin's daughter wanted to reach out to her father? (Stanza 12) If yes, why?

Answer Yes, she wanted to reach out to her father but she also wanted her lover with him. Thus, the girl stretched one arm towards her father and one arm round her lover. It shows that the girl neither wanted to die nor wanted to leave her lover.

Question 12. You are already familiar with the poetic device "alliteration". The poet makes extensive use of the same throughout the poem. Pick out as many examples of alliteration as you can.

Example Fast fatber's; horsemen-hard

Answer Examples of alliteration are

(i) "His horsemen hard behind us ride"

(ii) "My bonny bride"

(iii) "Stormy sea"

(iii) A down the glen

(v) Storm and shade

(iv) Water wild went

(vii) Left lamenting

Question 13. What is the rhyme scheme of the poem?

Answer ab ab is the rhyme scheme of the poem.

Question 14. Imagine you are one of the chiefs of the cavalry riding behind Lord Ullin. You and your men ride for three days at the end of which you reach the shore. Narrate your experience as you witnessed a father lamenting the loss of his child, in the form of a diary entry.

Answer

9 pm

26th April, 2012

Today at last after three days, we reached the shore with great difficulty. The wind was blowing horribly. The sea was raging. The waves rose higher and higher. Lord Ullin's daughter was trapped in the stormy sea. She was calling her father for help. Her one hand was stretched toward her father and the other was round her lover. Inspite of being so powerful he was unable to do anything. He was crying bitterly. Soon there was no sigh of Lord Ullin's daughter and her lover. The scene was heart-moving. I became upset to see the wailing at a father for his poor child.

Question 15. Imagine that you are Lord Ullin. You bemoan and lament the tragic loss of your lovely daughter and curse yourself for having opposed her alliance with the chieftain. Express your feelings of pain and anguish in a letter to your friend.

Answer

Invincible Castle

Scotland

5th February, 2012

Dear Glen,

You will be pained to know that my daughter is no more. I have no right to live any more as it was my fault to set my armed men to catch her and her lover. I should have given my assent for her marriage with her lover. I am the murderer of my bonny and beautiful daughter. She was drowned in the stormy sea infront of my eyes. She stretched her arm for help but I could not save her. I remember her innocent face crying for help. God will never forgive me. I am responsible for the tragic end of my daughter. I shall never forgive myself.

Lord Ullin

Question 16. In pairs, argue in favour of or against the topic "Lord Ullin's daughter was right in her decision to defy her father." Give logical and relevant reasons and present your point of view to the class.

Answer

For the Motion

Lord Ullin's daughter was right in her decision to defy her father. Love is very essential for life. It is a gift of God. It is not something that is at someone's command. She knew what was good for her. She loved the Chieftain very much. So, she eloped with her lover and nothing was wrong in their eloping together as her father would have got slain them.

Love is something that must not be denied at any cost. Lord Ullin could not understand the mood of the everchanging time. He failed to understand the generation gap. His daughter knew her father would kill her and her lover too. To me nothing was wrong in Lord Ullin's daughter to defy her. If she had been wrong, her father could not have asked her to return. She thought it better to sacrifice her own life.

Against the Motion

Lord Ullin's daughter was not right in her decision to defy her father. Parents know what is good for their children and they love their children to the maximum. She would have thought that her step would spoil the reputation of her father.

In this kind of situation, a girl should always talk to her parents. The parents have got better experience of the life. It is the moral duty of the children to respect the feelings and emotions of their parents. But Lord Ullin's daughter did something wrong in defying her father. She also ruined the social status. She should have persuaded her father and sorted out the matter.

5

The Seven Ages

William Shakespeare

Synopsis

The poet compares the world to a theatre stage and the people living in the world to the players of theatre. He explains how the players on the stage of the world plays various roles during various stages of their lives. The poet tells that every character has his fixed entry and exit. There are total seven ages of life.

Detailed Summary

First Three Stages of Life

The first stage is the stage of infancy. At this stage, a person does not know to speak and thus cry for all its requirements. Moreover, he often gets sick at this stage. The second stage is of adolescence when the child goes to school unwillingly while making noise, moving, slowly and carrying a school bag at his back. The third stage is of an adult/a lover. Who is singing the sad ballads while remembering his mistress.

Fourth Stage of Life

At this stage, one converts to a soldier. He has strange oaths taken by himself for various achievements. He is bearded like a leopard. A person at this stage is jealous of others and quite impatient. He may fight at quickly on small issues of honours also. He is not afraid of danger or death at this stage. However, this wordly reputation is hollow and temporary like a bubble.

Fifth Stage of Life

Then the fifth stage is the stage of judgement. Here, the man judges the rights and wrongs in the life. He grows fat, round and fleshy like a fat chicken. He has harsh looking eyes, formal cut beard. He wisely looks around at the instances and develops wisdom in his sayings.

Sixth Stage of Life

At this stage, a man is leaned down. He wears slippers and loose pants. He wears spectacles and his skin becomes loose. To keep his little things, he keeps a pouch tied to his belt. The clothes of his young age are very loose for his shrunk and thin legs. His loud mainly voice turns to childish trebles. He makes whistles while he speaks.

Last Stage of Life

Last scene of one's life is his last scene in the theatre of world. This ends the whole life full of events. A man becomes like a child at this stage who forgets everything, his teeth are gone, his eye sight goes away, he cannot taste things and later one day everything goes away.

About the Poet

William Shakespeare was born in 1564 and died in 1616. He was born in Stratford-upon-Avon. He is an English poet, lay night and considered one of the greatest dramatists even today. He is often called England's national poet and the Bard of Avon. He wrote 154 sonnets, two long narrative poems and about three dozen plays. He perfected the dramatic blank verse and used poetic and dramatic means to create unified aesthetic effects. His work has made a lasting impression on world theatre and Literature. In Shakespeare's day, English grammar, spelling and pronunciation were less standardised than they are now and his woe of language helped shape modern English.

Exercises

Question 1. What according to you, are the stages of a person's life? What characteristics would you assosite with each stage? (*e.g.*, childhood, innocence, joy)

Answer

Stages of Life	Characteristics
Childhood	Innocence, Joy
Adolescence	Stress, Fun, Jealousy
Youth	Work, Fun and Attractions
Middle Age	Responsibilities, Understanding, Maturity
Old Age	Understanding, Relaxation, Forget fatness

Question 2. On the basis of your understanding of the poem, answer the following questions by ticking the correct choice.

(a) All the world's a stage is an extended Metaphor for
  (i) the life shown in well known plays
  (ii) seeing the well known plays
  (iii) life of well known actors
  (iv) life of man that comes to an end

Answer (iv)

(b) All 'have their exits and their entrances'. Exits and entrances refer to
  (i) birth and death
  (ii) beginning and end of play
  (iii) coming and going of actors
  (iv) the end of the Shakespearean era

Answer (i)

(c) The seven roles that a man plays correspond to his
  (i) chronological age in life
  (ii) desires
  (iii) mental age in life
  (iv) idea of a perfect life

Answer (i)

Question 3. Having read this extract, identify the stages of a person's life as Shakespeare has done. Write down these stages in your note book, and sum up characteristics of each stage in two or three words, *e.g.*,

Stage	Characteristic Feature
Infancy	Crying, weak, dependent

Answer

Stage	Characteristic Feature
Infancy	Crying, weak, dependent
Adolescence	Complaining, Properly dressed
Adult	Smartly dressed, sad, moody,
Soldier	Temperamental, hard working, ambitious, fearless, decisive
Head of the family	Wise, protective, sincere, thoughtful, responsible
Old age	Thin, leaned, weak
Senile	Teethless, poor eyesight, tasteless and forgetful

Question 4. Work individually, and rank the seven stages in order of attractiveness. If you think being a school boy is most attractive, you could rank it number-1. Then, work in groups of four and compare your individual rankings.

Answer

Stage	Rank
Infancy	2
Adolescence	1
Adult	3
Soldier	4
Head of family	5
Old age	6
Senility	7

Note *Ranking will depend on individual outlook for life.*

Question 5. Explain the meanings of the following

(a) " .... all the men .... and their entrances".

Answer Every human being on the Earth is mortal. Each person is like the character of plays. They have their own assigned roles in life. When a child borns, he or she enters in the play of life. Going through different stages of life, he plays different roles in life. At last, a human's exit of play of life occurs by death.

(b) "And then the lover,

Sighing like furnace ...."

Answer A lover is like a furnace filled with love for his mistress or with frustration of inability of meeting her. When he faces the distance from his beloved he sighs like a furnace.

(c) "a soldier,

.... seeking the bubble reputation

Even in the cannon's mouth."

Answer A person becomes ambitions as a soldier. He seeks even for the transitory reputation and also he risks his life for them. He knows that he may die. He is temperamental, ambitious and energetic at this stage.

Question 6. You already know the two literary devices generally used by writers for comparison, *i.e.*, metaphor and simile. *e.g.*

(a) He was a lion in the battle, (metaphor)
(b) He fought like a lion, (simile)

In (a) the writer talks of the soldier in terms of a lion. The comparison is implied. In (b) the writer compares the soldier to a lion with the use of the word like, (as may also be used for such comparisons.)

Read the poem again and note down the metaphors and similes. Copy and complete the following chart.

Item	Metaphor	Simile
World	All the world's a stage	
Men, women		
School boy		
Lover		
Soldier		
Reputation		
Voice		

Which comparison(s) do you find most interesting? Why?

Answer

Item	Metaphor	Simile
World	All the world's a stage	—
Men, women	All the men and women merely players	—
School boy	—	Creeping like snail, unwilling to school
Lover	—	Sighing like furnance
Soldier	—	Bearded like the pard
Reputation	The bubble reputation	—
Voice	Childish treble	—

The most interesting is the Metaphor where human beings are compared to players of a drama. Poet has described mortality, the truth of life in a very interesting way. All the human have their set roles like players in the play. We enter on the stage of world with our birth and exit with death.

Question 7. In this poem, life is compared with a play. Just as in a play, a man acts many parts, so also in life, a man plays many roles. Can you think of some other comparison for life? (For example, life could be compared with the seasons in nature, the days of the week, the lessons in a school day.) Select one of these comparisons (or choose one of your own), and write about the similarities that life has with it. (80-100 words)

Answer

Similarities of a Tree with the Stages of Life

Birth Tree comes out as a small plant with tender and shining leaves. Human being is born with shining eyes and soft body.

Childhood As a small plant needs care and protection, a small child also needs the same.

Youth The child grows into tall, nice human being who starts benefitting his family financially and by loving the members. A tree also grows to give fruits, shade to the people around it.

Old Age As in old age a human is unable to work and care, similarly a tree also becomes unable to provide fruits, leaves, and therefore it provides no shade.

They, then wait for death which ends everything.

6

Oh, I Wish I'd Looked After Me Teeth

Pam Ayres

Synopsis

The poetess Pam Ayres regrets neglecting her teeth in the poem. She has eaten lot of sticky sweets and toffees but she has not brushed her teeth properly. Now, she has to suffer the pain on the dentist chair. She used to laugh on her mother's false teeth and now she would herself wear false teeth. The poem is a fine warning to the children who do not brush properly and eat lots of sweets. It is a humorous poem about keeping one's teeth in good health.

Detailed Summary

Poetess' Wish

Poetess wishes that she had looked after her teeth and could spot the danger earlier. She says that she should have taken proper care of her teeth but she did not. She said that she ate lots of toffees, sweets, gobstoppers and did not pay attention to her falling teeth. She wished that she would have bought something different from these sweets. Whenever she thought of lollies, liquorice, tiny and big sweets, hard peanuts, her conscience got pricked due to repentence.

Poetess' Brushing Habbits

She never gave up sweets, though she brushed her teeth and checked them. She did not do anything good for her teeth. She had to undergo injections, fillings, drillings etc.

Poetess' Visit to Dentist

The poetess sat on the chair of dentist and had to look in despair while the drill worked on into her mouth. She was to get two fillings.

Price of Neglecting Teeth

The narrator remembers of her mother's denture that was foamed in the water. Narrator had to pay the prices of eating candies, toffees, sweets etc. She had to lose her teeth. She wished she had looked after her teeth when it was the time.

About the Poetess

Pam Ayres was born on 14th March, 1947. She is an English poetess, songwriter and presenter of radio and television programmes. In June 2004, she was awarded the MBE for services to literature and entertainment. She worked with BBC Radio in various programmes. She is a keen gardener and a book keeper. Her biography **'The Necessary Aptitude : A Memoir'** was published in 2011.

Exercises

Question 1. On the basis of your reading of the poem complete the following table

Answer

Stages in the Life of the Poet	Activities	Consequencs
Youth	Eating toffees, sweet sticky food, gobstoppers, liquorice, sherbet, dabs, peanut brittle etc.	Cavaties, decay, caps
Adulthood	Eating gobstoppers, liquorice, peanut brittle etc.	Visit to dentist and false teeth

Question 2. On the basis of your understanding of the poem, answer the following questions by ticking the correct choice

(a) The title *'Oh, I Wish I'd Looked After Me Teeth'*, expresses

(i) regret (ii) humour (iii) longing (iv) pleasure

Answer (i)

(b) The conscience of the speaker pricks her as she has

(i) been careless (ii) been ignorant

(iii) been fun loving (iv) been rude

Answer (i)

(c) The speaker says that she has paved the way for cavities and decay by

(i) eating the wrong food and not brushing

(ii) not listening to his mother

(iii) laughing at his mother's false teeth

(iv) not listening to the dentist

Answer (i)

(d) The tone of the narrator is one of

(i) joy (ii) nostalgia (iii) regret (iv) sorrow

Answer (iii)

Question 3. Answer the following questions.

(a) 'But up and down brushing'
And pokin' and fussin'
Didn't seem worth the time-I could bite!"

What do these lines convey?

Answer In these lines, the poetess described that she did not follow a proper pattern of brushing the teeth. She did not brush her teeth by moving the brush up and down in all the right directions. She did not give reasonable time to her teeth while brushing at night. She did not control herself eating various kinds of sweets. She thought her teeth are alright, but these were in the process of decaying.

(b) Why did the poet go to the dentist? How could she have avoided it?

Answer The poet went to the dentist for the treatment of teeth by the process of drilling, filling or injection. She could have avoided this by eating less chocolates and sweets and by brushing them properly and regularly.

(c) "If you got a tooth, you got a friend", what do you understand from the line?

Answer It means that a tooth in mouth is a friend who helps us in chewing food. If there is no tooth in mouth, one becomes friendless.

(d) With reference to the poem, how can you look after your teeth?

Answer We can look after our teeth by avoiding eating chocolates, toffees, sticky sweets etc. It is also necessary to brush our teeth properly and regularly.

(e) Give an appropriate proverb that conveys the best message that this poem carries.

Answer Healthy and sparkling teeth.
Add lusture to your health.

Question 4. Listen to the conversation between Doki and his sister, Moki. As you listen complete the idioms and expressions listed below.

1. Sleep ....
2. .... me the willies
3. Crack the ....
4. Take the .... to water
5. .... tail.
6. Wonders will ....
7. .... can't be undone.
8. Reap what I ....

Answer
1. Sleep **a wink**
2. **Giving** me the willies
3. Crack the **nut**
4. Take the **horse** to water
5. **Turn** tail
6. Wonders will **never cease**
7. **Past** can't be undone
8. Reap what I **had sown**

Question 5. Read the following statement were 'I' refers to 'you.' "I can't afford to, after what Jack's done to his teeth."
What is it, you think you can't afford and why? Write a diary entry of not less than 125 words.

Answer

25th September, 2012

9:00 pm

It was so bad to see Jack with decaying teeth. He had sparkling white teeth earlier. But now his cheeks have also misformed due to loss of teeth. It has ruined his personality. I can't afford to loose my teeth like that. Healthy teeth leads to healthy body whereas decaying and diseased teeth leads to bad breath.

There are number of germs that get accumulated to the mouth. I cannot take up the terror by sitting on the dentist chair. So, I have decided to take good care of my teeth. I will now avoid eating junk food and eat healthy food. I will brush my teeth properly to make my teeth sparkling like pearls. Not much hard work in required for that.

Just Think

Question 6. In line 35, the poet has misspelt the word 'amalgum'. Why do you think she has done that? Discuss.

Answer Suggested points for help during discussion

(i) To suggest miss pronunciation due to tooth decay.
(ii) To add humour to reader.
(iii) To add horror to patient.
(iv) To add rhythm to poem.
(v) To suggest cantion in the reader's mind.

7

Song of the Rain

Kahlil Gibran

Synopsis

The poem 'Song of the Rain' written by 'Kahlil Gibran' which shows the personification of rain. Rain in the poem tells its story and its effects on the nature. The falling of the rain has a welcome song in it which everybody can hear but only few understand it. Rain is defined as the 'sight of sea' 'laughter of the trees' and the 'tears of heaven'.

Detailed Summary

Personification of Rain

The rain has been personified in the whole poem. It says that it is like dotted silver threads that drops from heaven by God. Nature adorns her fields and valleys with rain. Rain calls itself as beautiful as pearls which has plucked from the crown of Ishtar, God of fertility, love, war etc by the daughter of Down to adorn the gardens.

Rain and Its Effect

Rain says that when it falls heavily then hills laugh loudly because they get refreshed due to it. When it is a bit slow, flowers rejoice and make merry. When it bows, everybody and everything becomes happy.

Rain as a Messenger

Rain says that between the two lovers *i.e.,* fields and the clouds, it is a messanger of mercy. It quenches the thirst of the fields and relieves the clouds from the sickness caused due to water vapours that puff them.

Rain Like Cycle of Earthly Life

The arrival of rain is announced by the thunder and the departure of rain is announced by the rainbow. Its life is also like the earthly life who comes and goes, takes birth and dies. The rain says that it emerges from the water vapours of sea and moves to sky with breezes. Whenever it feels that field need it, it falls down and embraces the trees and flowers in millions of ways.

Understanding of Rain and Various Aspects of Rain

Rain says that it knocks everybody's window with its soft fingers and sings its welcome song. However, only sensitive people are able to understand those songs. Rain describes itself as the breath of the sea, laughter of the fields and tears of the heaven which is full of love, colours and spirit which brings heaven of memories for all.

About the Poet

Kahlil Gibran was born in year 1883 and died in 1931. He was a Lebanese American artist, poet and writer. In Arab world, he was regarded as a literary and political rebel.

His romantic style was at the heart of renaissance in modern Arabic literature. He is chiefly known in the English-speaking world for his 1923 book 'The Prophet'. While most of Gibran's early writings were in Arabic, most of his works published after 1918 were in English. He was an accomplished artist, especially in drawing and water colour. He was buried in Mar sarkis Monastery in Lebanon and later it became the 'Gibran Museum'.

Exercises

Question 1. (a) Given below are five lines from a poem but they are not in the right order. Get into groups of four. Read the lines and put them in the right order. Read the version that you develop to the whole class.

The voice of thunder declares my arrival.
I emerge from the heart of the sea.
I descend and embrace the flowers.
I am dotted silver threads dropped from heaven.
The rainbow announces my departure.

Answer The correct order is

I emerge from the heart of the sea.
The voice of thunder declares my arrival.
I am dotted silver threads dropped from heaven.
I descend and embrace the flowers.
The rainbow announces my departure.

(b) What is 'I' in these lines?

Answer 'I' refers to the rain in these lines.

Question 2. On the basis of your understanding of the poem, answer the following questions by ticking the correct choice.

(a) The rain calls itself the 'dotted silver threads' as
(i) the shimmering drops fall on after the other
(ii) it ties haven and Earth
(iii) it dots the Earth with shimmering water
(iv) it decorates the fields

Answer (ii)

(b) The tone and mood of the rain in the poem reflect its
(i) love for the Earth (ii) desire to take revenge
(iii) merriment as it destroys (iv) desire to look beautiful

Answer (i)

Question 3. Answer the following questions.

(a) Why is the rain divine?

Answer Rain is divine as it falls from heaven from the crown of God Ishtar and brings love and happiness for people, quenches the thirst of earth and makes the field fertile.

(b) In this universe rain performs many functions. What are those?

Answer Rain adorns the gardens and valleys. It makes hills laugh and embraces the flowers and trees. It quenches the thirst of earth and makes the land fertile. It cures the clouds who are overloaded by the water vapours. It provides joy to everybody and everything in the nature.

(c) "When I cry, the hills laugh;

When I humble myself the flowers rejoice;

When I bow, all things are elated".

Cry, humble and bow indicate different intensity with which the rain falls. Explain the three in context.

Answer 'Cry' means when it rains heavily. 'Humble' means when it rains modest and light. 'Bow' means very light rain.

(d) How do you think the rain quenches the thirst of the fields and cures clouds ailment?

Answer When rain falls on the dry field they become fertile and crops grow in it. Moreover, rain releases clouds from the overburden of water vapours. Clouds, after rainfall, become light and relaxed.

(e) Think about millions of little ways in which rain embraces the trees. Mention a few of them.

Answer 'Rain embraces the trees' is a metaphor used in the poem. Rain covers the tree with water and washes away all dust and soil. Due to which its leaves glisten and they look fresh. Moreover, rain makes the roots of the trees strong and provide all the nutrition to it. It provides strength and energy to trees. It becomes source of life for the trees.

Rainfall also promotes the growth of new small trees which has grown as plants. It provides them water by which they get energy to grow faster. It feels as if the rain hugs all the trees and plants, and give its love and affection to them.

(f) "....... All can hear.

"...... All can hear, but only the sensitive can understand sensitive can understand."

What does the poet want to convey?

Answer The poet wants to convey the idea that everybody hears the sound of rain when it falls. However, only few sensitive people enjoy that sound and feel the value and need of rain in the life. Rain brings joy, happiness, freshness and love for all those who realise.

(g) (i) Notice the imagery built around 'sigh of the sea', 'laughter of the field' and 'tears of heaven'. Explain the three expressions in context of rain.

Answer Rain rises from the sea in the form of water vapours. These water vapours form clouds. Due to precipitation, the vapours get converted into rain and falls back to earth. Fields get water and become fertile. This fertility supports the growth of plants on fields and everyone becomes happy. The rain becomes the drops of the heaven as it brings happiness and prosperity on earth.

(ii) How would you express rain as

an agent of flood?

a source of water for dams?

Answer Rain becomes an agent of flood when it rains heavily nonstop for days together and this unexpected rain overflows the river and the water comes to cities, towns and villages. Earth is also unable to sustain that water. Flood causes lots of miseries to all.

Rain water is properly channelised in the dams and therefore rain becomes the source of water in dams. Then, as per the needs and requirement, dam water can be properly used. Dam water is used for making electricity, irrigation and drinking purposes.

(h) "I am like earthly life ..".

Why does the poet call the rain as earthly life?

Answer The poet calls rain as earthly life. As on earth we all emerge and die, Similarly, rain also emerge from the sea, and then fall back to earth before death. The life on earth also goes through birth and death process.

(i) Explain the ending of the song.

Answer The ending of the song is like farewell to all with love. The rain recollects its various aspects. They are 'sigh from the sea', 'laughter from the fields' and 'tears due to endless memories of time.

Question 4. 'Ode to Autumn' is a beautiful poem written by the famous poet John Keats. Listen to an excerpt from the poem and pick phrases which personify autumn.

Phrases

....	....	....
....	....	....
....	....	....
....	....	....

Answer Few phrases are as follows

(i) bosom friend of the maturing Sun

(ii) sitting on the granary floor

(iii) riper of fruits etc.

Question 5. Rain in the hills and rain in the desert present entirely different scenario. In the hills it revitalises the greenery and freshens the vegetation; it waters the parched land and relieves the thirsty and panting souls in the desert.

This has been year of scanty rains. Imagine how the rain would be welcomed when it pours in the hills and in the desert after a long dry spell. Choose one of the places and describe

(a) What are you likely to see?

Answer Rain always comes with joy after a dry spell. When rain comes, soil absorbs it and soon the hills and deserts change their dry look. In a hilly area, it presents a green and refreshing colour. In deserts, earth starts changing its dull colour to greenish with vegetation coming up in the fields. The scanty vegetation of the desert looks fresh and greenish also. The temperature comes down. The dry environment becomes refreshing. Everybody enjoys the greenery and freshness all around.

(b) What would happen to the rain water?

Answer The lakes are full of water after the rain. Nature takes the help of rainwater to beautiful her fields and valleys. People become busy with the process of rainwater harvesting.

(c) What would be the scene before and after the rain?

Answer Actually rain is regarded as a messenger of love, mercy and blessings. It quenches the thirst of the fields. It embrace all kinds of vegetation, giving it a new lease of life. After rain, earth gets its power to sustain all kinds of life. The dry and uncomfortable environment is replaced by all-round greenery, beauty and freshness. Everybody welcomes rain with an open heart and enjoys the pleasant ambience.

Drama

2

The Bishop's Candlesticks

Norman Mckinnell

Synopsis

'The Bishop's Candlesticks' is a popular play written by Norman Mckinnell. It shows the supermacy and victory of love and kindness over hatred, ill-will and narrow-mindedness. Side by side, the story of the play reflects how the mind of one convict changes due to love and kindness of the Bishop. The play gives the message: "our poor body is the temple of living God."

Detailed Summary

Marie and Persome

Marie worked as a maid at the house of Bishop. She was stirring soup on the fire. Persome was upset as she did not know where her brother has gone the Bishop after 11'o clock. Marie told her that Bishop has gone to her mother because she was feeling poorly. Persome asked her to put salt cellars on the table. Marie told that Bishop has sold the salt cellars for Mere Gringoire. It was because she could not pay rent. Persome felt very bad and thought that the Bishop would sell everything for the sake of others.

Bishop Enters the Home

The Bishop entered the home and told Marie that her mother was feeling better now. Persome angry with the Bishop. She said that any clever person could dupe him. The Bishop said that there was so much suffering in the world and he cannot do much for everyone. The Bishop is taunted by her as she said that one day he would sell the candlesticks also which were given by his mother. Bishop answered on this that he never wanted to sell them.

Convict Enters the House

At midnight when the Bishop settled down to read, a convict entered in the house and asked for food on the point of a knife. The Bishop gave him food to eat. The convict ate it like a beast. Persome is, however frightened to see the knife in the convict's hand. The convict told the Bishop that he was living in hell for the last ten years. He told his sad story to the Bishop. He told him that he had a lovely wife and a beautiful home. One day, his wife was ill and he had no money or work to feed her. He stole food but got caught by the police. He was sent to jail for ten years.

Convict's Life in Jail and His Escape

He was beaten mercilessly in jail and was chained like a wild animal. He was not even fed appropriately and covered with vermin all around. If he complained, he was beaten more. One day they forgot to chain him and he got the chance to escape. He was called by a number in the prison. The Bishop asked him to sleep as there was the couch.

Silver Candlesticks

The convict looked at the candlesticks greedily. The Bishop left the convict and went to sleep himself. The convict stole the candlesticks, hid them in his coat and ran away. Suddenly, Persome woke up, and shouted loudly when she saw that the candlesticks were gone. She asked the Bishop to inform the police but he did not want the convict to be in prison again. So, he stopped Persome from calling the police.

Convict Brought Back by the Police

The convict was brought back by the sergeant and the three policemen. They told that the convict was moving suspiciously. On searching him they found the candlesticks on him. The Bishop looked at the convict and recognised him as a good friend. He honoured him to dine last night and he himself gave him those candlesticks as a gift. The sergeant freed the convict and went away.

Convict Changed to a True Christian

The convict was changed by the incident. He became shamefaced. The Bishop asked the convict to sleep. He told him that he had to go Paris. The Bishop gave him those candlesticks and said that these might help him. He even told him the safe passage to Paris. The convict was overwhelmed by the Bishop's attitude. The Bishop has made him feel like another man now. He felt himself as a man and not a beast. The Bishop said, "our poor body is the temple of the living God."

About the Writer

Norman Mckinnel was a scottish stage and film actor and playwright. He was born in 1870 at Maxwelltown. He became known over the course of his career for playing many Shakespearian roles. He was also known for writing several easily-stageable one-act plays, the most successful of which was 'The Bishop's Candlesticks' (1901). Mckinnell died of a heart attack in London in 1932.

'The Bishop's Candlesticks' is an adaptation of a section of Victor Hugo's "les miserables". It is widely considered one of the greatest novels of the 19th century. It is considered as one of the longest novels (fourteen hundred pages in unalridged edition) of all time.

Exercises

Question 1. What would you do in the following situations? Give reasons for your answer.

(i) If you were travelling by bus and you saw someone pick another passenger's pocket.

(ii) If you found a wallet on the road.

(iii) If you were in a shop and you saw a well-dressed lady shoplifting.

(iv) If your best friend is getting involved with an indesirable set of friends.

(v) If you were in school and you saw one of your class-mates steal another child's pen.

Answer When we discuss the topic in groups there may be various answers. Here one view point is given

(i) I would raise an alarm so that thief is arrested.

(ii) I would return it to the nearest police station.

(iii) I will ask her not to do this, otherwise I will inform the respective authority.

(iv) I will advise my friend and make him conscious about what he is doing.

(v) I shall scold the boy and tell him not to do it any more.

Question 2. Imagine a child has been caught stealing in school. In groups of eight play the roles of

- The child caught stealing
- The child she/he stole from
- The teacher
- The headmaster
- The witnesses

Try to find the reason why the child stole and the possible advice you can give her/him. Should the child be punished? Or should she/he be counselled?

Answer The class teacher will guide the students to perform the play. Some important hints to be followed are

(i) We should hate the sin, not the sinner.

(ii) We should help the sinner to be a reformed person.

(iii) We must know the reason behind the crime. Basic needs sometime make us criminals. We should try to solve the root cause of the problem.

(iv) We should tackle the situation sympathetically. Love, compassion make wonders on everybody. With the help of these, we should try to convert the criminal.

Question 3. Copy and complete the following paragraph about the theme of the play in pairs.

The play deals with a ____(I)_____ and ____(II)_____ Bishop who is always ready to lend a _____(III)_____ hand to anyone in distress. A ____(IV)_____ breaks into the Bishop's house and is ____(V)______and warmed. The benevolence of the Bishop somewhat _____(VI)_____ the convict, but, when he sees the silver candlesticks, he ___(VII)____them, and runs away. However, he is ____(VIII)______ and brought back. He expects to go back to jail, but the Bishop informs the police they are a ____(IX)_____. The convict is ____(X)_____ by this kindness of the Bishop and before he leaves he seeks the priest's blessing.

Answer

(I) convict	(II) a	(II) helping
(IV) convict	(V) given food	(VI) changes the heart of
(VII) steals	(VIII) caught	(IX) gift given to him
(X) converted		

Questions 4. (a) Working in pairs give antonyms of the following words.

kind-hearted unscrupulous forgiving stern benevolent credulous generous pious suspicious sympathetic understanding wild innocent penitent clever brutal cunning caring sentimental trusting protective concerned honourable embittered

Answer

kind-hearted	—	cruel, unkind
unscrupulous	—	scrupulous
forgiving	—	unforgiving
stern	—	sentimental
benevolent	—	hard-hearted
credulous	—	incredulous
generous	—	miserly, mean
pious	—	impious
suspicious	—	unsuspicious
sympathetic	—	unsympathetic
understanding	—	inconsiderate
wild	—	civilised
innocent	—	guilty
penitent	—	unrepentant
clever	—	innocent
brutal	—	kind-hearted
protective	—	unprotective
honourable	—	dishonourable
cunning	—	simple hearted
caring	—	careless
sentimental	—	stern
trusting	—	untrusting
concerned	—	uncon cerned
embittered	—	softened

(b) Select words from the above box to describe the characters in the play as revealed by the following lines from the play.

	Lines From the Play	**Speaker**	**Quality Revealed**
1.	"You told him she was feeling poorly, did you? And so my brother is to be kept out of bed, and go without his supper because you told him she was feeling poorly."		
2.	...... "take my comforter, it will keep you warm."		
3.	"If people lie to me they are poorer, not I."		
4.	"You are like a child. I can't trust you out of my sight. No sooner my back is turned than you get that minx Marie to sell the silver salt-cellars"		
5.	"My dear there is so much suffering in the world, and I can do so very little."		
6.	"My mother gave them to me on - on her death bed just after you were born, and ....and she asked me to keep them in remembrance of her, so I would like to keep them.		
7.	"I am too old a bird to be caught with chaff."		
8.	"You have your soul to lose, my son."		
9.	"Give me food or I'll stick my knife in you both and help myself."		
10.	"... they have made me what I am, they have made me a thief. God curse them all."		
11.	"Why the devil are you kind to me? What do you want?'		
12.	"I - I - didn't believe there was any good in the world. . .but somehow I - I - know you're good, and - and it's a queer thing to ask, but could you, would you bless me before I go?"		

Answer

	Lines From the Play	Speaker	Quality Revealed
1.	"You told him she was feeling poorly, did you? And so my brother is to be kept out of bed, and go without his supper because you told him she was feeling poorly."	Persome	stern
2.	...... "take my comforter, it will keep you warm."	Bishop	kind, caring
3.	"If people lie to me they are poorer, not I."	Bishop	caring, understanding
4.	"You are like a child. I can't trust you out of my sight. No sooner my back is turned than you get that minx Marie to sell the silver salt-cellars"	Persome	protective, concerned
5.	"My dear there is so much suffering in the world, and I can do so very little."	Bishop	kind, caring and concerned
6.	"My mother gave them to me on - on her death bed just after you were born, and ....and she asked me to keep them in remembrance of her, so I would like to keep them.	Bishop	sentimental, lovable
7.	"I am too old a bird to be caught with chaff."	Convict	clever, cunning
8.	"You have your soul to lose, my son."	Bishop	sympathetic, caring, concerned
9.	"Give me food or I'll stick my knife in you both and help myself."	Convict	brutal, pitiless
10.	"... they have made me what I am, they have made me a thief. God curse them all."	Convict	STET, embittered
11	"Why the devil are you kind to me? What do you want?'	Convict	Wild, suspicious
12.	"I - I - didn't believe there was any good in the world. . .but somehow I - I - know you're good, and - and it's a queer thing to ask, but could you, would you bless me before I go?"	Convict	repentent, sentimental

Question 5. Answer the following questions briefly.

(a) Do you think Bishop was right in selling the salt-cellars? Why/Why not?

Answer Yes, Bishop was right in selling the salt-cellars. This shows that people mattered more to him than worldly materials. Moreover, Bishop was a kind-hearted man who always rendered his help to the needy people.

(b) Why does Persome feel the people pretend to be sick?

Answer Persome is not as kind-hearted as Bishop. She thinks that people pretend to be sick, so that Bishop can help them financially and they can earn from him.

(c) Who was Jeanette? What was the cause of her death?

Answer Jeanette was the wife of the convict. She was ill and died due to starvation, her husband could not bring food for her. At that time, the convict had no work or money. He stole food but police caught him and sent him to prison.

(d) The convict says, "I am too old a bird to be caught with claff." What does he mean by this statement?

Answer The convict meant that he has spend a long period of his life in jail. He has learned all the tricks and, now he cannot be cheated by any kind of softness of words. He is old enough for this.

(e) Why was the convict send to prison? What was the punishment given to him?

Answer The convict was sent to prison for stealing food. He was chained like animals and beaten like hound. He was not given proper food and had vermins on his body. Due to the ill-treatment of police he had turned into a wild beast.

(f) (i) Do you think the punishment given to the convict was justified? Why/Why not?

Answer I think that the punishment given to the convict was not justified. The convict had only stolen food for his ill wife. At the most, the law should have fined him or imprisoned him for a short time. But rigorous imprisonment for ten years was too much for the man who has stolen only food to eat.

(ii) Why is the convict eager to reach Paris?

Answer The police would be after the convict to arrest him again as he has not completed his sentence. He was eager to reach Paris because he would not be easily traced by the French police.

(g) Before leaving, the convict asks the Bishop to bless him. What brought about this change in him?

Answer Bishop's love, large heartedness, care and kindness brought the change in the convict. Bishop saved him from the police. He has now changed to a gentleman from a beast. Therefore, he asked Bishop to bless him so that he could stay like this forever.

Question 6. Read the following extract answer the questions that follow by choosing the correct options.

(A) Monseigneur, the Bishop is a ... a hem!

(a) Why does Persome not complete the sentence?
(i) she used to stammer while speaking.
(ii) she was about to praise the Bishop.
(iii) she did not wish to criticise the Bishop in front of Marie.
(iv) she had a habit of passing such remarks.

Answer (iii)

(b) Why is she angry with the Bishop?
(i) the Bishop has sold her salt-cellars.
(ii) the Bishop has gone to visit Mere Gringoire.
(iii) he showed extra concern for Marie.
(iv) she disliked the Bishop.

Answer (i)

(B) She sent little Jean to Monseigneur to ask for help.

(a) Who sent little Jean to the Bishop?
(i) Mere Gringoire
(ii) Marie
(iii) Persome
(iv) Marie's mother

Answer (i)

(b) Why did she send Jean to the Bishop?
(i) so that he could pray for her.
(ii) as she knew that he was a generous person.
(iii) as she was a greedy woman.
(iv) as she was a poor woman.

Answer (ii)

(C) I offered to take her in here for a day or two, but she seemed to think it might distress you.

(a) The Bishop wanted to take Mere Gringoire in because

(i) she was sick.
(ii) she had no money.
(iii) she was unable to pay the rent of her house.
(iv) she was a close friend of Persome.

Answer (iii)

(b) Persome would be distressed on Mere Gringoire's being taken in because ________

(i) she did not want to help anyone.
(ii) she felt that Mere Gringoire was taking undue advantage of the Bishop.
(iii) she was a self-centred person.
(iv) she would be put to a great deal of inconvenience.

Answer (ii)

Question 7. The term irony refers to a discrepancy, or disagreement, of some sort. The discrepancy can be between what someone says and what he or she really means or verbal irony. The discrepancy can be between a situation that one would logically anticipate or that would seem appropriate and the situation that actually develops or situational irony. The discrepancy can even be between the facts known to a character and the facts known to us, the readers or audience or dramatic irony.

Working in groups of four complete the following table. Find instances of irony from the play and justify them.

Extract	Justification
I believe you want to convert me; save my soul, don't you call it? Well, it's no good ___ see? I don't want any damned religion.	Later, the convict says, "it's a queer thing to ask, but- could you, would you bless me before I go".
• ________________________ ________________________ ________________________	• ________________________ ________________________ ________________________
• ________________________ ________________________	• ________________________ ________________________
'Why the devil do you leave the window unshuttered and the door unbarred so that anyone can come in?'	If the door had been barred the convict couldnot have entered the house.

Extract	Justification
• ______________________ ______________________ • ______________________ ______________________	• ______________________ ______________________ • ______________________ ______________________
My mother gave them to men on ___ on her death bed just after you were born, and ___ and she asked me to keep them in remembrance of her, so I would like to keep them.	Later he hands the convict the candlesticks and tells him to start a new life.
• ______________________ ______________________ ______________________ • ______________________ ______________________	• ______________________ ______________________ ______________________ • ______________________ ______________________

Answer

Extract	Justification
I believe you want to convert me; save my soul, don't you call it? Well, it's no good ___ see? I don't want any damned religion.	Later, the convict says, "it's a queer thing to ask, but- could you, would you bless me before I go".
But, Persome, the traveller in hungry.	He called the convict, a traveller and showed love even when he show knife.
I was *i.e.,* sentenced to ten years in the prison hulks, ten years in hell.	The convict called the jail as hell due to its suffering.
'Why the devil do you leave the window unshuttered and the door unbarred so that anyone can come in?'	If the door had been barred the convict couldnot have entered the house.
Ah, you are good, sister, to think of that, but I don't want to sell them.	Bishop did not want of sell them but he gave them to convict in the end.
They feed you in hell, but when you escape from it you starve.	This shows the problem of the convict and compulsion for him to stay in jail.
My mother gave them to men on ___ on her death bed just after you were born, and ___ and she asked me to keep them in remembrance of her, so I would like to keep them.	Later, he gave the convict the candlesticks and told him to start a new life.
"This gentleman is my very good friend".	The convict stole the silver candlesticks. Even after that the Bishop saved him from the police.

Question 8. Identify the situations which be termed as the turning points in the convict's life?

Answer

(i) The first situation was when the convict was caught by the police for stealing food for his ill wife.

(ii) The second situation was created by police by torturing him mentally and physically and made him a beast.

(iii) The third situation was that he met with the Bishop and transformed into a different man by the love of the Bishop.

Question 9. The convict is the product of society he lived in, both, in terms of the suffering that led him to steal a loaf of bread, as well as the excessive sentence he received punishment for his "crime". He was imprisoned for stealing money to buy food for his sick wife, this filled him with despair, hopelessness, bitterness and anger at the injustice of it all.

Conduct a debate in the class (in group) on the following topic. ***'Criminals are wicked and deserve punishment'.***

Answer Classroom activity but some points are given for the help.

S.N.	For the Motion	Against the Motion
1.	Criminals should be punished highly so that others can take a lesson.	Punishment is not a permanent solution. To forgive puts an impact.
2.	There is no chance of reformation for the criminals.	Reformation is required. It works always.
3.	Criminals are like the wild animals. They should be treated accordingly.	We should hate the crime, we should not hate the criminals.

Question 10. The convict goes to Paris, sells the silver candlesticks and starts a business. The business prospers and he starts a reformatory for ex-convicts. He writes a letter to the Bishop telling him of this reformatory and seeks his blessings.

As the convict, Jean Valjean, write the letter to the Bishop.

Answer

Jean Valjean Reformatory

Paris

24 March, 2012

Dear Godfather,

I hope you remember your ex-convict whom you changed as a nice-loving man. It was the turning point of my life when I first met with you. You are the noblest soul on earth and God for me.

I sold these candlesticks and have started a started a rehabilitation centre for the ex-convicts. This centre try to make their life better by giving them chances to do something for their own livelihood, My centre is doing well and I am satisfied with the honest earning of us. Some NGOs are also helping our organisation. I cannot tell you, how peaceful my mind is now. This is all because of you. You have made me what I am now. I am glad to inform you that I am arganising a programme for our centre. The reason is that the government has sanctioned a huge grant for us.

I would be glad, if you come and join as a chief quest during the programme. The programme is on April 15, 2012 at 6:00 PM. Please honour me by attending our programme. Seeking your blessings.

Yours Sincerely

Jean Valjean

www.ingramcontent.com/pod-product-compliance
Ingram Content Group UK Ltd.
Pitfield, Milton Keynes, MK11 3LW, UK
UKHW021657190726
13853UKWH00001B/321